Mister Leprosy

Mister Leprosy

by

PHYLLIS THOMPSON

HODDER AND STOUGHTON
AND
THE LEPROSY MISSION ENGLAND AND
WALES

British Library Cataloguing in Publication Data
Thompson, Phyllis
  Mister Leprosy
    1. Browne, Stanley George
    2. Missionaries, Medical – Biography
    3. Leprosy Mission – Biography
266′.025′0924   R722.32.b/

ISBN 0-340-25837-3

Foreword

I stood at the door of The Leprosy Mission in Portland Place, wondering why no one came to open it in answer to my ring on the bell. I'd been invited by the Executive Director, the Rev. R. J. Findlay, to come along and discuss the possibility of writing the story of Dr. Stanley Browne's fight against leprosy, and as I waited, looking at that door, someone mounted the broad step up from the pavement and stood beside me. It was a man of medium height, medium build, medium colouring, dressed inconspicuously in a neutral shaded raincoat, the sort of person who would pass unnoticed in a crowd anywhere in London.

'The door is open – it just has to be pushed hard,' he said pleasantly, and added as he held it back for me to pass in, 'Would you be Miss Phyllis Thompson?' Somewhat surprised that he should know me, I admitted that was my name. He gave a quizzical little smile as he announced casually,

'I'm Stanley Browne.'

So he had been invited to the discussion, too! It was my first encounter with the man who I later learned was world famous in the field of leprosy, whose opinions on the subject were sought by governments, whose name alone was an open sesame to leprosaria anywhere and everywhere. Its very ordinariness and friendliness were re-assuring. Nothing awe-inspiring about this eminent man. 'I was just a boy from an ordinary family in New Cross,' he said modestly. His achievements were due to *Dieu – et mon droit*. In that order.

Over an informal lunch of sandwiches and coffee with the Executive Director it was agreed that if Hodder and Stoughton would publish the book, I should write it.

So many of Dr. Browne's friends and colleagues, as well as members of his family, responded to my request for information concerning him that I should not know where to begin or end if I tried to acknowledge my indebtedness to each one individually. I am deeply grateful to them all. However, mention must be made of the Rev. Charles Attwater of The Leprosy Mission. He not only lent me various booklets and pamphlets and a copy of *Bonganga* by Peter and Sylvia Duncan (now out of print) which was rich in descriptions of Yakusu, but also supplied me with copious notes of his interviews with Dr. Browne. His help and that of his secretary, was invaluable.

More than to any, I am grateful to Dr. Browne himself, whose unfailing readiness to provide information, to answer my questions, and to check each chapter of the MS. as it was written, was a tremendous encouragement to me. Any deficiencies or inaccuracies in this brief sketch of his life and his fight against leprosy are entirely the fault of the writer.

Phyllis Thompson
June 1980

To
Mary and Vicky
Whose friendship I have treasured
since the time the three of us
lived together,
and to
Flora
Whose open heart and open home
Have enriched my life,
I dedicate this book

Contents

Prologue

There was something almost sinister about the silence of the forest, with only the occasional plop of a heavy raindrop, or the snapping of a twig to break the oppressive stillness. The leafy branches of the giant trees effectively shut out the glare of the sun, so that the three travellers on the sodden ground far below moved in a sort of dull-green twilight. If Stanley Browne, cycling single file with two Africans, had been given to morbid ruminations he could have imagined a hundred malevolent eyes were silently watching him, and the fancy would at least have prepared him for the horror that lay before him.

As it was, however, his attention was focussed on the narrow path along which he was proceeding cautiously, conscious that the slightest deviation could land him in the mud, to the hilarious amusement of his companions. He could hold his own with anyone at dodging the traffic up the Old Kent Road, but evading half-hidden roots or slimy patches in an equatorial forest demanded a different technique. The humid heat was sapping his energy, too, but he wobbled on cheerfully enough, for he was strong and healthy and accustomed to exerting himself.

'How much farther, Lofanga?' he called out to the youngster following him, though he knew what the answer would be before he asked. When it came it told him nothing.

'Don't know, *Bonganga*!' He gave a wry grin and continued pedalling, dismounting every now and then to carry his bike over a fallen tree or a wide stream. The journey seemed interminable.

Then, suddenly, he gave a shout, and stopped so abruptly that Lofanga bumped into him. The scene had changed, and they found themselves standing in bright sunlight, flooding down on them out of a metallic sky. The path they were following had led to a forest clearing, and they had come on it so unexpectedly that they stood blinking for a full minute, shading their eyes from the dazzling light and looking around bewildered.

Then they saw the huts.

They were roughly made and roofed with the usual thick palm fronds as in any other of the African villages they had passed through. But there was something different about these huts. They were low, no higher than a table, and out of them creatures were crawling, not walking, scarcely distinguishable in colour from the ground.

The two Africans looked uneasily at their white companion.

'Come on, *Bonganga*,' they murmured. 'This isn't the place to stop. We must get along . . .'

But *Bonganga* remained there, gripping the handlebars of his bicycle, staring at the human beings with their distorted faces who were crawling or hobbling towards him, holding out stunted hands, begging for food.

'Come on, *Bonganga*. Let's go. There's nothing we can do for them. It's the bad leprosy.'

But still *Bonganga* did not move. So this was the answer to the question he had so often asked, why it was that with so much leprosy about he never saw people in the advanced stages. It had puzzled him, for he knew enough about the disease to recognise when a patient at one of his clinics had the lepromatous form of leprosy that would lead on to damage to the nerves of limbs and face, with its deformities, its trophic ulcerations.

The Africans had another name for it. 'It's the mother of the bad leprosy,' they muttered when they discerned, quicker than the white doctor for all his book knowledge, the tell-tale gleam in the skin when the light glanced on it. But when he had asked, 'Where are the people with the bad leprosy?' the only reply he had received was a shrug of the shoulders, and an evasive 'Who knows?'

Now he knew. Banished into the forest to fend for themselves. Subsisting on berries and roots and such living creatures as they could catch in clumsy traps made with deformed hands. Outcasts. Victims of the mysterious disease that didn't kill, but condemned people to this sort of living death instead.

They were converging on him now, and with his quick doctor's eye he saw beyond the untended ulcers, the nodules, the fallen nose-bones, the stumps of hands and feet, and discerned the individual men and women, some old, some only teenagers. There were even some children.

Hopelessly they stood around him. 'Food! Food!' they pleaded, though it was obvious he had none.

He had spoken many times in the open air before, confronted various audiences, from supercilious onlookers in the Strand to hecklers in Bermondsey, but never had he felt so unprepared as now. What could he say to these people whose physical need was too appalling to ignore, for whom the future held nothing but to rot to death here in this forest clearing?

He longed to give them the ultimate message. 'This life isn't the end of it! There's a life beyond the grave, and there's One there Who loves you! He died to open the door to everlasting life in everlasting happiness—to you.'

This was no time for history or theology, far less for rhetoric. All he wanted to do was to tell them of the Son of the Most High God. 'His name is Jesus. You can't see Him, but He can see you. You can't hear Him, but He can hear you. Call on Him, believe in Him now, and He will be with you right to the end—and beyond . . .'

But the words would not come. Even if they had come, even if he had been able to speak as fluently there in the deep forest as he had spoken on village greens in England, these pathetic beings would not have understood. All their minds could grasp was that here before them was a white man, a member of that privileged class that always had enough and more than enough to eat. They hoped for nothing more than a little food, now.

'I haven't got any food,' he said stumblingly. 'But I won't forget you. I'll do what I can . . . I'll do what I can to help you,' he promised as he rode away.

The encounter had lasted less than fifteen minutes, but forty years later he remembered it as if it had just occurred. He did not realise it at the time, but the promise he made then was not so much to that little group of hopeless leprosy sufferers in the Topoke forest as to all leprosy sufferers in the whole world. He would do what he could.

The doing of it was to take him into spheres of which, as a boy from a side street in London, he had never dreamed, before heads of state and to international fame. Through deep waters of personal anguish too. A call had reached him that day which drew him on to the fulfilment of his own destiny, the purpose for which he had been born.

When I grow up I want to be a mish . . . mishon . . .
mishonary . . .

S.G.B.
Aged 5

CHAPTER ONE

Home at New Cross

A couple of German chemists experimenting in their laboratory.

A baby boy born in a working-class district in south-east London.

The two apparently totally unrelated events took place at the same time, although over thirty years were to elapse before they merged. The chemical compound that the chemists eventually produced lay unused for decade after decade on the shelves in research laboratories, while the baby grew to childhood, boyhood, manhood, and embarked on the career that led him first to a remote mission hospital beside the River Congo, then to the ends of the earth. This is his story.

Stanley George Browne, second son of his parents, was born on 8 December, 1907, near where the Old Kent Road runs into New Cross, and where, incidentally, one of the beacons was lighted four centuries before to warn London of the approach of the Spanish Armada. Rows of newly-built terraced houses now climbed the hill leading up to the site of the beacon, and into one of these the Brownes had moved from Bermondsey when they married. A sturdy, cheerful, hard-working couple were the Brownes. It was two and a half miles' walk through dreary streets from New Cross to Bermondsey, but they walked the distance, back and forth, twice every Sunday, for they were members of the Drummond Road Baptist Church there, and it was the spiritual centre of their lives. One of Stanley's earliest memories was sitting up in the rostrum (beside his father who, as Church

Secretary, always took his place next to the minister), and peering down at the congregation through the wrought-iron fancy grill. The privilege was only accorded when he was good, and didn't last long anyway, since as soon as he was old enough he had to sit among the other children in the front rows.

He went to Sunday School in the afternoon, too, along with his brother Frank, so that meant walking to Drummond Road and back twice. They grumbled about it to each other sometimes, but it was part of the pattern of their lives, the same as grace before meals, and a bath on Saturday night and clean clothes on Sunday. Later on, when their father provided them with bicycles, the tedious journey was transformed into a pleasant adventure.

In view of the smallness of the Brownes' income and the size of their family (another boy and two girls were born in the little house in Bousfield Road) it was remarkable that the boys had bicycles at all, for there were no well-to-do relatives to produce handsome presents at birthdays, and the salary of a Post Office clerk in those days left little over for luxuries. The fact that the whole family had an annual seaside holiday was probably due to the abstemious way in which the father himself lived. None of his money went on tobacco, nor was it spent in the convivial atmosphere of the public house to which so many working men converged on a Saturday night. There were no visits to music halls, either. He even begrudged tram and bus fares when they could be saved, and many was the time he walked from New Cross to attend a meeting at Drummond Road Baptist Church after a hard day's work rather than pay for public transport. He needed the money for his family, and for his regular contributions to his church.

His wife was one with him in all his Christian activities. Before their marriage she had been secretary of the Sunday School with its eight hundred children, and although this responsibility was relinquished when the claims of her growing family absorbed most of her time, she added to her household duties the making of one hundred pounds of marmalade every year. This was not only for home consumption, but to provide her husband with something to take when he went to visit members of the church who were sick. Her days were busy from morning to night at the wash-tub and the mangle, sewing, mending, darning, shopping and scrubbing, peeling potatoes and washing vegetables, sleeves rolled up as she plunged her hands into the flour bowl, kneading and moulding the dough. But the table was always laid punctually for meals, and the children were expected to take their places round it with their hair tidy and their hands and faces clean. As soon as their legs were firm enough to carry them they were given their appointed household tasks, and she taught them all, boys as well as girls, to cook.

'Our home life at New Cross was most happy,' Stanley wrote many years later. 'All my memories of childhood are of benign, yet firm, Christian influence. Strict by present-day standards, if you will, but certainly most happy.' It was a very close-knit family, in which respect and loyalty were indispensable ingredients. When Mr. Browne's father died and his mother was bereft not only of husband but of home, there was no serious question as to where she should live. The three-bedroomed house in Bousfield Road was the obvious place for her, and she was welcomed into it. 'She was a saintly woman, who had a remarkable memory. She had family tragedies, too, losing five of her seven children in infancy, my father and his younger brother being the sole survivors. She had a wonderful clear Christian testimony that I remember to this day. She passed away in 1923.'

Perhaps it was from her that he inherited his own encyclopaedic memory into which information and impressions were quickly absorbed, precisely classified, and readily produced when required. It was as though he had a vast and expanding mental store-room which his energetic mind was eager to fill. As a child he was for ever asking questions and applying facts with a disconcerting accuracy, so that to the irritation of his brothers and sisters he invariably won their childish arguments. 'Oh, Stanley's always right!' they would remark peevishly. What made it even more annoying was that Stanley knew he was always right.

His thirst for learning revealed itself early. When his brother Frank, two years his senior, was sent to school and returned home to relate what he had been taught, Stanley demanded to be sent too, and cried so persistently that his parents eventually succumbed. Soon after the age of three he was already enrolled as a pupil in the near-by Elementary School, the youngest child there.

His father, at any rate, understood this innate desire for knowledge. Although he had left school at an early age, he had been keen on furthering his education, and attended night schools, becoming so proficient in French that he was sent on postal journeys to Paris and Switzerland. His crowning triumph in this field was to be appointed official translator into English at the International Postal Congress in Paris. Stanley was only four at the time, but listened with rapt attention as his father related some of his adventures on arriving in the French capital.

'I had to go to a street called the *Rue de Lille*,' he explained. 'So I asked several people, and they all said there was no such place. At last I showed someone the address in writing, and immediately there were smiles all round, people waving their hands about, telling me where the place was. You see, I'd pronounced it wrong. I'd said Roo de Lil, instead of *Rue de Lille*,' and here he pursed his lips, carefully enunciating the sounds, 'and they could not understand my English accent!' It was the little boy's first lesson in the language in which he was later to become as fluent as in his own. '*Rue*', he said, 'Not roo. *Rue* . . .' When French pastors whom his father had met came to the house, he listened to them as they talked, trying to understand what they were saying.

One of the visitors in those days was a member of the Aborigines Protection Association which was exposing the atrocities perpetrated in the Congo—an early introduction to the part played by the great powers in international politics.

Stanley, rather surprisingly, did only moderately well at Elementary School. He was not a model pupil, nor was he a model son. 'Wayward, headstrong, disobedient', were some of the epithets he later used to describe himself in those days. Many a Sunday dinner, usually a very happy time with the whole family gathered around the table, was clouded for Stanley's tender-hearted little sisters who knew that he was in for a stiff caning as soon as it was over. However richly he may have deserved his punishment, the fraternity of childhood was reinforced by their affection for the brother who was always willing to carry them pickaback on family outings. Stanley never suffered from the sense of embarrassment some boys feel at being seen about with small sisters, and would carry little Ivy on his shoulders for miles, never seeming to tire. Furthermore, he was willing to play with them from time to time, though the game invariably took the form of 'doctors and nurses' rather than 'fathers and mothers'. Stanley, of course, was the doctor, but Winifred was allowed an important role as the nurse, while the diminutive Ivy took the place of the indispensable patient, was bandaged up, carried around, and given horrible-tasting concoctions to swallow as medicine. Such favours bestowed weighed heavily with the girls, and the swish of the cane as it came down on Stanley's behind had them gasping in sympathy. What if he had been turned out of some childrens' meetings held in the local Methodist Church because his behaviour was so bad? What if he had been reported for disobedience and insolence at school? Ooh! That must have hurt! Poor Stan!

When he was eleven he had to sit for an examination which, if he passed, would qualify him for Grammar School. He failed to gain an entry there, but was admitted, instead, to a Central School at Brockley.

These Central Schools were provided for children who

had failed to gain entry into Grammar or Secondary Schools, but were above average academically. Brockley Central School already had a reputation for producing successful scholars. The headmaster was a man who knew each of his pupils personally, boys and girls alike, assessing their abilities, encouraging talent when he saw it, firm, magnanimous, respected by staff and scholars into whom he inculcated a deep sense of pride in their school. For Stanley it was a transition from childhood to boyhood as he entered a world in which the best was expected of him, where all were encouraged to strive for the mastery in the classroom and on the sports field, where discipline was strict and loyalty imperative. He quickly got to know the characteristics of the teachers—Miss Ingram, always referred to privately as 'Inky', with her long, sweeping skirts, shirt blouse and tie, excitable little Madame Valette Vernet, who enlivened the French lessons by slapping recalcitrant pupils when she was cross, Miss Harris whose face coloured with embarrassment when her class played up, Mr. Rankin the art master with a walrus moustache, who was always being asked to put something in autograph books, and Mr. Lyon, his very popular sports and class master, whose sudden death as the result of a road accident cast a gloom over the whole school, and prompted Stanley to write:

> On Thursday last, fourteenth of May
> Our friend and teacher passed away
> . . . Beloved of all he was, but then
> How oft 'tis said of such fine men
> As flowers are plucked when in full bloom,
> So these come early to their tomb!

In due course this poetical tribute appeared in the school magazine, over the name that was already becoming well known. Stanley Browne seemed to figure high up on all the lists in class and in sport, and achieved distinction when he won first prize in the whole school for an essay on a true incident in his life. One who knew him in those days described him.

'He was very fair, had very slightly prominent teeth, a fresh complexion and looked altogether a very healthy young schoolboy. He was shy and sensitive, given to blushing occasionally. His prowess at sport, cricket, fives, etc., was of no less a high standard than his ability in class. He was usually top of the boys' section in examination results.'

It was early in his time at Brockley Central School that he became aware of his unusual inherent ability. 'I found that if I worked I could succeed. In the first year I came top of the class and was top in nearly every subject. The next year, too. I found that if I exerted myself I could excel in any subject to which I put my hand, and began to see how foolish it was to kick against the pricks.'

He wanted to do well in life. He was beginning to taste the sweetness of success as week after week he heard his name read out as coming top of the class in this subject and that, and ambition was born. He must work for what he would attain, but if he worked he could attain it. Work! Very early in his life he was developing the capacity for diligent, painstaking study and the ability clearly and promptly to communicate his findings, and he started doing it in a home-made shed in the little back garden.

This shed, which was made with Frank's help out of old cartridge boxes left over from the First World War, became his study. Morning after morning, then evening after evening, he was to be found there, poring over his books. Winifred was made responsible for keeping it clean and washing the curtains, so she was allowed to use it sometimes, but by common consent it was Stanley's room. He even had a morse code system by which he could be in touch with those in the house! 'Idleness wears out quicker than work,' an adage gleaned from a French folk story of two plough-shares, one rusty the other shining, caught his imagination and he did not hesitate to quote it on occasion. Not that idleness ever characterised the Browne family in Bousfield

Road, or that any of the children skipped their homework. Every evening, as soon as the tea things were cleared away, silence descended on the house as they opened their satchels, drew up chairs to the table, and settled down with their exercise books. The only difference with Stanley was that he studied longer, got up earlier in the morning to do it, and took more subjects than the others.

It was taken for granted that Stanley was the one who worked the hardest, with Winifred running him a not too close second.

So the years passed, with tension and excitement added when in 1914 war was declared on Germany, and files of khaki-clad men marched through the streets down to the Channel boats, when huge, sausage-shaped Zeppelins moved heavily across the sky, dropping bombs, and one occasionally crumpled up in a blaze of flames when hit by anti-aircraft fire. Mr. Browne, a T.B. suspect, was exempted from the military call-up, so the family was spared the strain of separation and sorrow so many endured in those days, as news reached home after home of husband, brother, son being reported missing, or killed in action, or taken prisoner. But in 1921 he was ill for a long period, then was involved in a road accident which put him in hospital for seven months on half pay. Voluntary contributions from his colleagues helped to augment the Browne's slender income, but it was a period of anxiety and hardship for them all, accompanied by many fervent prayers. When Harold and Ivy suddenly came out in spots which were diagnosed as scarlet fever, and taken off to isolation hospital forthwith, it was seen, not as a disaster but a deliverance. It meant two fewer mouths to feed for several weeks! Frank, as the eldest, had to leave school early and start work, and Stanley must do the same thing as soon as a suitable job came along. His headmaster knew the family circumstances, and when Stanley was fifteen he urged him to apply for the post of junior clerk in the Town Clerk's department at the Deptford

Town Hall. There was a vacancy there, and he recommended Stanley.

'You'll be Town Clerk one of these days, Stanley,' he said hearteningly.

Stanley was dismayed. 'I'd hoped I could finish my fifth year here,' he said regretfully. 'I wanted to finish . . .' To leave before he'd taken his final exams, and relinquish the prospects that might follow! 'I wanted to finish.'

The head looked understandingly at the lad. This was his star pupil, and he was sorry to see him go. Before they parted he quietly gave him some advice.

'Stanley,' he said. 'There are three things you'll need to know as you go through life.' He paused, then added slowly,

'Know men.' He spoke from experience, for he knew his pupils, their characters as well as their talents, their weakness as well as their strength. That was why he was able to help them. He went on,

'Know the Bible.' He paused again, and added,

'Know God.'

Stanley was arrested, for it was unexpected. This was no stimulus to gaining academic knowledge. The emphasis was on something deeper, more profound, reality in a different sphere. He stood silent, letting the words sink in, then nodded.

'Yes, sir,' he said. 'Yes. I'll remember that. Thank you, sir.'

They shook hands, and he went out. He had left his schooldays behind.

* * *

Through the warp and woof of those first fifteen years of his life had been woven a sort of golden thread, the significance of which emerged later. Brought up as he was in a home where the Bible occupied a place of supreme importance, where the necessity of repentance towards God and faith in our Lord Jesus Christ was constantly affirmed, where prayer and piety went hand in hand, it is not surprising that his first consciousness of a Divine calling should have come at a very early age.

He was five years old when the Reverend Lorraine arrived at Drummond Road Baptist Church one Sunday, and in addition to preaching to the adults spoke to the Sunday School. As he told of some of his adventures as a missionary pioneering in the Lushai Hills of North India the children listened breathlessly, none more eagerly than little Stanley Browne, who went home from Sunday School that day with his head full of what he had heard. What a wonderful man! And what an exciting life he had!

It so happened that the following day at school his teacher told the children to write a composition on 'What I want to be when I grow up.' Stanley sat at his desk, head on one side, and started to write,

'When I grow up, I want to be a . . .' then sat biting his pencil. He had come to a halt. He knew exactly what he wanted to say. The difficulty was that he did not know how to spell the word 'missionary'. Sixty years later he still remembered wondering what were the right letters to use.

'I don't guarantee that I spelt it correctly, but that was the first glimmering that missionary service might be the culminating motive of my life.'

Away in China in the midst of revolution, a missionary couple were rejoicing in the birth of their first child—a girl. In Africa, by the Congo River, a small dispensary had just been opened by Baptist missionaries in a village called Yakusu. Both were to be woven into the tapestry of his days by a Master hand, though the threads were still so far removed from each other. Meanwhile, the little boy grew and developed, giving no evidence at all of having received a Divine call—rather the reverse, in fact, some of his teachers would have said when they saw him mockingly mouthing the very words they could not think of as they tried to express themselves. His quick brain had raced ahead of theirs, and now like an evil little gnome was turning and laughing at them. No, young Stanley Browne was too clever by half, and it was a pity he didn't put his talents to better use than making fools of his elders! 'The borderline between a joke and impertinence is very narrow,' he was told. 'Write that sentence fifty times, adding the words, "I overstepped it." '

Then another missionary came across his pathway, this time from Africa. The Rev. Henry K. Bentley had the distinction of being the first white baby to be born in the Congo, where he was in considerable danger of becoming a juicy morsel in a cannibal stew-pot. Again Stanley was deeply stirred by all that he heard, and during the course of the week of meetings, Mr. Bentley took the boy aside and had a talk with him. His father and mother were Christians, each knowing Jesus Christ as personal Saviour — but what about their son Stanley?

Stanley admitted that he wasn't a Christian, that he hadn't asked Jesus to come into his life. Yes, he had heard many times that Jesus would forgive anyone who confessed his sin and asked for pardon, but he hadn't really done it himself. Yes, he wanted to. He wanted to become a Christian. So Stanley prayed, admitting that he had done many wrong things, being frequently disobedient and cheeky, and asked God to forgive him and make him His child. For Jesus Christ's sake. Amen.

And when, at the final meeting, the missionary asked who would be willing to follow Jesus, even to the Congo, Stanley's hand was one of those that went up.

Outwardly it didn't make much difference, and those who looked hopefully for signs of permanent improvement were disappointed. After a few days, when the freshness of the experience had waned, he went on much as before, the only difference being that inwardly there was an uneasy feeling that he was on the wrong side again. His intensified energy in study was largely due to the realisation that it was foolish to continue 'kicking against the pricks'. Not until a Christian Endeavour Society was formed at his church which he, as a son of the Church Secretary, felt compelled to join, did he come to life as a follower of Jesus Christ.

The Christian Endeavour provided just the sort of atmosphere in which the inspiration of a life lived for God could be presented in relevant language, for it was a society for young people led by young people. The weekly meeting included Bible study, extempore prayer, and the open expression of personal Christian experience as they were encouraged to talk freely together. If you have no personal Christian experience to speak about—*why* not? You've got to be a true follower of Jesus Christ if you want to be in the Christian Endeavour! And you must learn to preach, to proclaim the Gospel, for He's told us to go into all the world and do it, and the place to start is right here. And the time is now!

The fervour and the reality of it, the uncompromising challenge to commit one's whole life to God's service, wherever and however He should direct, the pledge taken in all solemnity to do so, and to make a start by undertaking to attend C.E. regularly—well, the seeds sown in Stanley's young heart over the years all seemed to spring to life now. To the steady, earnest, enthusiastic devotional exercises of those C.E. meetings and what he learned in them he often attributed the quickening in his spiritual life that set him on the pathway of true discipleship.

The significant thing about it all is that the church in Drummond Road was without a pastor at the time, and the area in which it stood was on the very border of some of the worst slums in London. The men and women of the church were almost entirely from working-class homes, few if any had gone to college, some of the older ones were almost illiterate. Yet there was a warmth and a depth in the fellowship of that church that produced lasting results in the lives of many of the young people connected with it.

In November, 1922, the year in which Stanley enrolled as a C.E. member, he was baptised along with twelve others, including his brother Frank.

Although only fourteen, he was already developing into an eloquent speaker, and it dawned on him that this was gift given to him by God, along with his ability to succeed at whatever he put his hand or mind to, providing he was prepared to work. The following year he gained first place in all England in the Sunday School Union Scripture examination.

'It's all come from God,' he said determinedly. 'And it's all going back to God.'

His days and his evenings were full. He was head boy at school, vice-captain of both swimming and cricket, he was studying for several Society of Arts exams, and in addition to that planned to enter for the all-England Scripture Competition. He was satisfied and happy, and when his parents received a grant of £15 per annum for him he was delighted that this would help to alleviate the financial pressure at home.

But it was not enough. Frank was already earning his living, working in the City, but with four healthy, growing youngsters still to be fed and clothed, the family income was insufficient to allow for extra schooling. Stanley must apply for the job at the Town Hall in Deptford, and if he was accepted it was understood he would leave school at once.

He got the job. His ability to take shorthand at the rate of 100 words a minute, with a typing speed of forty, double distinction in French and a smattering of knowledge of office routine, backed up by a respectful, pleasing manner and excellent references, carried the day in his favour. His salary would be fifteen shillings and five pence per week, he was told, and he should turn up for work on Monday, at 8.30 a.m. sharp.

Any temporary elation he may have felt at his success quickly subsided as he walked home, and gloom settled on him instead. By the time he reached the bottom of Bousfield Road his throat was feeling thick, and as he walked up the hill past the long row of identical little houses with their bay windows and small, privet-hedged front gardens to No. 77 the backs of his eyes began to sting. The tears could not be restrained, and when he got indoors they rolled down his cheeks as unashamed he sobbed out the news. 'They've taken me on. But oh, I don't want to leave school!'

NOT NEEDING WORDS

Young man, the challenge rings out loud and clear,
   As now the Saviour calls with tender voice:
Between the rival claims of ties most dear
   And service true, He bids you make your choice.

The countless multitudes who ne'er have heard
   The Gospel's joyful news of pardon free,
Unite to plead for God's redeeming Word:
   Shall their insistent call unanswered be?

Perhaps it is the sacrifice you dread:
   Home ties exert their strong restraining hold:
Ambition may be calling you to tread
   The pleasant path that leads to fame or gold.

But stay, the former voice is calling still:
   Your consecrated life the Master needs
In some far station you alone can fill,
   Where you may reinforce your prayers with deeds.

So now, when all your powers are in their prime,
   Consider first the Savour's rightful claim:
Surrender talent, energy and time
   For active service in the Master's Name.

S.G.B
Aged 17

CHAPTER TWO

Clerk in the Town Hall

It took exactly fourteen and a half minutes to walk the distance from home to Deptford Town Hall at the rate of four miles an hour, Stanley found out, and arranged his daily departure accordingly. His life was controlled by a strict, self-imposed timetable, and he arrived at the Town Hall each morning with unfailing punctuality, an inconspicuous figure of medium height, medium build, medium colouring, clad in a suit of medium quality, complete with stiff white collar and bowler hat. He was the perfect junior clerk in appearance as well as in manner, although his senior colleagues soon discovered that his ordinary exterior concealed a person with more than ordinary intelligence and enterprise. One of his duties was to collect sixpence a week from all members of the Town Clerk's staff and with this to provide them with tea and biscuits each afternoon. To everyone's surprise, he gave them all a refund at Christmas. Not for nothing had his mother taught him how to make tea so that the smallest amount of leaves would produce the greatest number of cups of tea, where to buy the best biscuits at the lowest price, and how to make a pint of milk go a long way.

'Young Stan's a bright boy,' they agreed, impressed by his enterprise as well as his efficiency in dealing with files, shorthand notes and typewriters. 'He'll go far, that lad. He'll be Town Clerk one of these days, will young Stanley Browne.'

As far as he was concerned the job at the Town Hall made no great demands on him, and he returned from it each day

31

fresh enough to spend his evenings in study. Four times a week he attended evening classes, enrolling for courses in the usual academic subjects including French and English, and in addition to these, shorthand.

There was a practical reason for taking an advanced course in shorthand. He saw it as a means of earning a livelihood while he put himself through university. To go to university! This was his ambition now, and since he could expect no financial help from anyone, it would be up to him to do what was necessary by his own efforts. If he could obtain a Shorthand Teacher's Diploma, that would enable him to get a job which he could do in the evenings, while he attended lectures during the day. It meant working hard and putting in long hours, but he was already accustomed to that. So he was up by 6 a.m. each morning, and his day assumed its usual pattern. A time to read the Bible and pray, then down to study until he was called for breakfast. Then off to his nine-to-five job at the Town Hall, home for tea and away again for the twenty-five minutes' walk to attend evening classes, or go to Drummond Road for church meetings there.

It was a very full life. Even on Saturday afternoons, when the Town Hall was closed, he had his programme planned. A young engaged couple who attended a local Anglican church had issued invitations to any young people owning bicycles to join the Cyclists' Evangelistic Band which they had formed. The purpose of this was to combine healthy exercise in the fresh air with open-air meetings rather like the Salvation Army though without the trumpets and tambourines. So off they went together, a high-spirited company of fellows and girls in their late teens and early twenties, cycling through the streets of south-east London to the leafy Kent or Surrey countrysides till they came to a village green where they dismounted, produced large posters for display, and started to preach to the people who sauntered over to see what was going on. Then, after a pause long enough to talk to anyone who showed an interest, off they went to the next convenient spot, to repeat the procedure. By this time Stanley was developing a quiet but authoritative manner of preaching, crisp and to the point, so that not only in the open air but at meetings in churches he was quite in demand as a speaker. 'The boy preacher,' he was sometimes referred to in Bermondsey.

Then there was his Boys' Own.

The history of his Boys' Own went back to the time when, in 1923, the Superintendent of the Sunday School at Drummond Road Baptist Church came to him about a class of particularly rebellious and unmanageable boys who had proved too much for three successive teachers.

'Stanley,' he said. 'I wonder if you can help me? I'm left again without a teacher for this class.' The boys were thorough-going young rascals, as mischievous as monkeys, he didn't deny that, and he was at his wits' end to know what to do about them. 'Would you be willing to take them on? You're young to do it, I know,' Stanley was fifteen at the time, 'but it might be an advantage for someone to teach them who's nearer their own age, yet just that much older to command their respect. How about it, Stanley?' So Stanley took them on, and decided he'd tackle the class in a different way. Instead of the usual type of Sunday School lesson based on a passage of Scripture, he told them the story of a missionary—Alexander McKay.

'And those Bermondsey boys actually listened! I can see them now, listening. I quoted from one of the biographies I had read in which Alexander McKay spoke about digging nuggets from the Word. And I remember being greeted at the end of the first month by one of those Bermondsey boys, 'Got any more nuggets, Mr. Browne?' and I said, 'Yes, and we're going to dig them out together!'

It was no small triumph, either, at the age of fifteen, to be respectfully addressed as 'Mr. Browne'!

His association with these boys resulted not only in a number of them becoming Christians, but in the formation of the club which Stanley called the Boys' Own. He organised outings for them, and later on took them for camping holidays at Shoreham in Sussex and Dymchurch in Kent.

Meanwhile the underlying desire to go to university urged him on in his studies, for until he had passed the Matriculation Exam he could go no further. Very well then. He would take the Matriculation Exam.

He had set himself a hard task but he was determined to accomplish it. He enrolled in evening classes for the necessary subjects, English, Mathematics, French, Physics and Chemistry, eager if possible to get through the whole course in one academic year. He wrote out in large letters on a piece of cardboard words to spur him on and put it on his desk.

Perseverance leads to success.
All things are possible to him that believeth.
L'oisiveté use beaucoup plus que le travail.

He wanted to remind himself what was required if he was to succeed. The family had moved to a larger house now, and he had a bedroom to himself, from which issued strange and pungent odours as he experimented with chemicals late into the night. Even on holidays and outings it was no unusual thing for him to be found sitting on a gate or the bough of a tree, earnestly perusing a study book he had slipped into his pocket. It all had to be done in his spare time, after he had fulfilled his commitments at work and at the church, for through it all those responsibilities in connection with Christian Endeavour and his class of boys were shouldered unfailingly. At one stage, convinced that there was insufficient interest in overseas missionary work among the young people in the church he started a study group for the subject. It was held at 7.30 a.m. on a Sunday morning, that being the only time a suitable room was available in the church, so it meant him leaving home at 7 a.m. in order to get to Bermondsey in good time to lead the meeting.

He often said in later years that he did not know how he

managed to pack so much into that formative period of his life. The fact that he was able to do so was due not only to his own inherent ability and his dedication, but also to the atmosphere of emotional and spiritual security in which he lived. The happiness of the home was sometimes clouded by illness and poverty, but never by any tension between parents or through favouritism shown to children. The five children all knew themselves to be loved, even when misdeeds were rewarded by a spanking, painful and unpleasant, but acknowledged to be just. They quarrelled among themselves, as children do, but let one of them be set on by anyone else and the other four were ranged alongside. Theirs was a very close-knit family life, and singularly uncomplicated, for the Browne's faith was simple and uncompromising in its outworking. As Christians there were certain things one just did not do. One did not waste money on smoking and gambling, one did not pander to the lusts of the flesh by drinking alcohol or flirting in dance halls, one did not grieve the Holy Spirit by using foul language or reading foul literature. One did not do these things, so why go where they were done? No point in praying 'Lead us not into temptation', if one deliberately went where temptation lurked! So there were certain places to which one simply did not go. And since, as Christians, there were so many things to be done, what with keeping one's body fit by healthy exercise, and one's mind by healthy study, enriching one's spirit by prayer and Bible reading, one's emotions by joyful fellowhip with God's people, all for the purpose of pleasing one's Master and being ready to help one's fellow men, the hours and the days were full. The children had each embraced the faith of their parents, so however one or another might flag from time to time, they were all facing in the same direction, understanding each other's aims and when need arose ready to help—or to correct with brotherly frankness. Talking about books with one of his young sisters one day, Stanley said decisively,

'You have to be selective. If you read this, you *don't* read

that!' There were some things in life towards which there
was only one attitude to adopt—cut it out! It might mean
one's friends regarded one as being namby-pamby at times,
but it saved one all the perplexity and heart-searching that
ensued when one had gone a little way in a dangerous
direction and wasn't quite sure when to stop. If one hadn't
even started, there was no problem!

Viewed from the permissive standpoint of the last quarter
of the twentieth century, the manner of life of evangelicals
like the Brownes in the years before the Second World War
was strict and narrow, evading the social issues of the day.
When seen on the broader canvas of world need, however,
it proved to be the workshop in which was welded not one
but two instruments destined to carry health and healing to
disease-ridden Africa (Winifred as well as Stanley became a
medical missionary), and in the case of Stanley himself
beyond that to victims of leprosy worldwide. The security of
the home that was always there, with its regular schedule,
its familiar faces and its family jokes, provided a retreat
where the single-minded student could pursue his studies
undisturbed by friction, controversial debates, or thought-
less interruptions.

One year at evening classes, and Stanley had completed
the whole course of study necessary to enter for the Matric.
In June, 1926, he sat for the Exam, walking back five and a
half miles to New Cross in the evenings, to save the fare. A
short time later it was recorded in the Minutes of the
Metropolitan Borough of Deptford,

'We report with pleasure that Mr. S. G. Browne, the
Junior Clerk in the Town Clerk's Department, has passed
the London Matriculation Examination, being placed in the
first division. As only 6 per cent of the total entrants obtained
a first-class pass, we feel sure that the Council will wish to
join with us in congratulating Mr. Browne on his outstanding
success.'

Stanley coloured up slightly as he received their congratu-
lations, and backed away modestly, but all the same he was

pleased to know that his achievement had been recorded in the printed minutes. It was the second time an educational success of his had received such honourable mention. The previous year it had been when he was awarded the Royal Society of Arts Bronze Medal for English, coming second in the whole country. The Metropolitan Borough of Deptford had expressed itself delighted. Furthermore, two local papers had reported it. Now once more he was in the news— very small items, it is true, but the little reports were worth keeping, and he stuck them in his scrap-book, along with the one about Winifred obtaining a scholarship. It was heartening to know of the approbation of others.

He was on the first rung of the ladder that led to university now, though the goal still seemed very far off. 'Perseverance leads to success,' he reminded himself, and enrolled for evening classes again as the new academic year opened in September.

'I'll do logic and philosophy and psychology, along with French and English,' he thought, 'and aim eventually for a London external degree.'

But things were moving in a realm of which he knew nothing, and purposes for him were ripening. The attention of the London County Council had been drawn to the increasing number of intelligent young men attending evening classes. Several of them had shown academic ability, and the question was asked, 'Can't something be done to encourage them to follow a course at a university?' The outcome of the discussion that followed was the decision to offer what was to be called a Non-Vocational Scholarship, which would allow the selected student a grant of ninety pounds per annum plus University fees for two years, in order that he could follow a course of instruction in Arts or Science in any college he should choose.

This was something new. Ambitious students in the evening classes took note, Stanley included. Young men with academic ability—didn't he come into that category, with his medals from the Royal Society of Arts and from the

National Union of Teachers, as well as a double distinction in French and Oral French?

The hitherto unthought-of possibility of becoming a full-time university student opened up before him and brought with it perplexity as well as hope. Even if he won the scholarship, the grant of ninety pounds would only be sufficient to pay for his food, his travelling and his books. There would be no difficulty about accommodation, of course. He could continue living at home, and he would be free to choose a college near enough to do so. The question was whether it was right for him to give up a job with good prospects at a time when his father was only just recovering from the effects of his accident, and continue living at home without making any appreciable contribution financially.

'I don't know what I ought to do,' he told the minister of his church. 'I want to go on with my studies. I feel the Lord has helped me — that He's given me these gifts and I ought to develop them. But it would mean that for at least two years I couldn't make any worthwhile contribution at home, and even if I got a degree, who knows how soon I'd get a job?

'I want to do the Lord's will. At least, as far as I know, it's what I want,' he added honestly. 'I've searched my heart and my motives, and I'm ready to apply for this scholarship or give up the idea altogether. But I still don't know. The Lord doesn't seem to have given any indication either way. What do you think I ought to do?'

The minister looked at him and shook his head.

'Stanley,' he said. 'I don't know either. He might be calling you to take a step of faith about finance and go ahead for the grant, trusting Him to provide. On the other hand, He might be calling you to a painful renunciation, to give up the thing you'd most like to do.

'You know, I'm not one who believes in asking the Lord for a sign,' he went on. 'I believe He wants us to find His way for us through the Scriptures, and the working of the Spirit in our own hearts, and through circumstances, too.

We walk by faith, not by sight. All the same,' he paused a moment, and Stanley looked at him expectantly.

'It seems to me this is a case where we can ask for a sign. You genuinely don't know what to do, and I can't help you. Let's ask God to make it clear, if you ought to apply for this grant, by doing something special. Some special blessing, some evidence of His power in your life that will convince you that you should take this step. Let's ask Him for a sign.'

So the two of them knelt and prayed. Oh Lord, give a sign, some special evidence of Thy blessing, that we may be assured . . .

Stanley went home and looked again at the application. He had already filled it in, and if he delayed much longer it would be too late, the opportunity would be gone. Yet without the confidence he was doing the right thing, he could not send it. 'Some special blessing,' Mr. Mitchell had said, 'as a sign you should go forward.' He must wait for the sign, whatever it might be.

The following Sunday evening he was booked to speak at a Girls' Brigade anniversary service in a Baptist church some miles away. There seemed no apparent connection between that event and his own particular problem, but as he cycled to his appointment he felt unusually conscious of the presence of God. He found himself praying as he sped along, unable very clearly to make a specific request but with a full heart yearning for a manifestation of divine power as he preached.

'Bless the message, Lord,' he prayed. 'And Lord – show me the way that I should take!'

Although he preached with exceptional fervour and conviction, nothing out of the ordinary seemed to happen. There were the usual warm-hearted handshakes as he stood at the door of the church while the congregation filed out, and several people thanked him for the sermon they had listened to, but there was no evident reason for the buoyancy and elation with which he rode home. And when Monday morning dawned, and he set off for Deptford Town Hall to start another week's work, he was still waiting for that special blessing that would confirm him in going ahead with the application for the scholarship. The feeling of joy he had experienced the day before had subsided, and everything was back to normal. Perhaps there was to be no sign after all. Perhaps it was the will of God that he should continue as a clerk in the Town Hall, and relinquish the prospect of being a full-time university student.

The days passed uneventfully. He had returned from work on Thursday evening, and was surprised when a knock on the front door revealed Mr. Mitchell standing there. From the glint in his eye, and the expression of subdued excitement on his face it was evident he had news to impart.

'Stanley,' he said. 'I've had a phone call from the minister of the church where you were preaching on Sunday evening. Something wonderful happened. He told me he knew of two people who came to Christ during the sermon, and this morning he heard of two more—one of them a young soldier who was in the neighbourhood just for the weekend.

'Stanley! We asked God for a sign. Some special blessing— and on Sunday night four souls were saved as you were preaching! Isn't this the confirmation you needed to go forward with that application?'

*   *   *

It happens not infrequently in life that a move in a new direction is accompanied by trials or crises from unexpected sources. With the rather solemn, though inspiring sense of being called by God to take the step of applying for the scholarship, Stanley might have anticipated things would go smoothly. As it was, however, the next few weeks were fraught with emotional strain, not so much because of uncertainty about his own future but because of the sudden illness of his mother. The persistent headaches and transient lack of vision that she had been enduring drove her at length to the doctor. Then she was admitted into Guy's hospital, and to the dismay of the whole family they learned that she had a cerebral tumour. It would mean an operation—obviously it would be a very serious one.

The day before the operation they all went to see her except Harold, who was away, and as she looked round at her children one thought was uppermost in her mind. Perhaps she knew that she had come to the end of her earthly life, and that only eternal things mattered now.

'You do belong to Jesus, don't you?' she asked them each one. When they looked into her eyes and said quietly, 'Yes, mother,' she was satisfied.

Early in the morning three days later Stanley was at the hospital. He was on his way to County Hall to be interviewed for the Non-Vocational Scholarship, and decided to go and see her first.

The news was very grave. She was unconscious, and was failing fast. At 9 a.m. she died.

He left the hospital immediately afterwards. He must hurry if he was to be in time for the interview. Mother was dead. The shock and the grief of it had to be stifled, and as he went in to face the officials and answer their questions he was conscious of being quietly upheld, as though by a strong, invisible Hand. So clear was his mind at the interview that he was able afterwards to remember every question he had been asked and the answers he had given.

The events of that momentous day were etched vividly upon his mind, leaving a lasting impression of the presence of God in the midst of sorrow and tension, and in the days that followed, in spite of the natural sense of loss of the one who had been the bulwark of the home, this consciousness remained. The pattern of life had changed, but the family pulled together, sharing the household responsibilities as best they could, and when the news was received that Stanley had been granted the Non-Vocational Scholarship and could start at King's College in the autumn, there was no suggestion that he should do otherwise than go ahead.

And they brought little children to Him, that He might touch them.
Mark 10.13

Give me Thy touch, O Master,
  That with Thy care and skill,
I may with hands devoted
  Attend the weak and ill.

Give me Thy great compassion,
  The smile, the heart of love—
Marks of the Great Physician,
  An unction from above.

Give me the 'vision splendid',
  In all my work to see
That helping little children
  May lead them, Lord, to Thee.

S.G.B.

(Written in the textbook Lectures on Diseases of Children *when he began his children's clerking at King's College Hospital in 1932. He gained the 'G. F. Still Prize for Diseases of Children' that year.)*

CHAPTER THREE

Student at King's

The newspaper reporter, instinctively aware of the unusual, crossed over the road at the corner of the Strand and the Aldwych, to see what was going on. A little crowd had gathered there, right outside the Gaiety Theatre, and he could see it wasn't a street vendor advertising his wares, or a tout offering a sure winner for the next big race, because a policeman was standing near by and making no effort to interfere. So it evidently wasn't an accident or a fight, either. The reporter, hoping for a story, joined the group of mid-day loungers, and saw they were gathered around half a dozen young men, dressed informally in sports coats and flannel trousers or plus fours.

'They are bare-headed, and wear multi-coloured neckties,' he wrote later, describing the scene. 'They are of the type that would run you, row you, jump you or box you. One of them is speaking—not ranting or declaiming or bellowing,' and to the reporter's surprise he hears words like 'salvation', and 'penitence', and 'the Lord Jesus Christ'. This is unusual, to say the least of it, and he cranes his neck to get a better view of the speaker.

'He has cropped, curly fair hair, a healthy open countenance and a wild necktie of school colours. He tells of his religious experience and of a life that something has changed. The small knot of people listens intently and silently and nobody seems to find in this public confession of a religious faith any matter for astonishment . . .

'The young man ends his simple testimony, without peroration, and steps back shyly. His place is taken by

43

another, who smiles frankly and ingenuously at his hearers. Then another and another. All speak of the same experience, an experience of something that has made a difference.'

The reporter is in luck, because just as one of the speakers is saying 'In Jesus Christ', there is an interruption, which provides him with more copy. An elderly, stout, rather breathless woman dressed in Salvation Army uniform steps forward, addresses the young fellows warmly as 'you dear men', and insists on saying something herself.

'Briefly, but with simple eloquence, and marking her emphasis with a stick, she adds the testimony of her seventy-three years, and the testimony of three score years and ten is found to be the same as that of eighteen. The story is the same in its simplicity, its faith, its hope and its burning conviction.' The reporter is moved by what he has seen and heard, and having found out that the young preachers are undergraduates from King's College, just across the way, he goes back to write it all up for the *Guardian*, concluding his report with the words,

> It takes a great deal of moral courage and an intense conviction to come out into the Strand at midday to bear witness to a belief in unseen things, but so long as such courage and such conviction are to be found in the young today, who shall say that the religion of the Cross is a spent force in our land?

Meanwhile the young men themselves hurry back across the busy thoroughfare, dodging the rumbling traffic and the chattering pedestrians, to sprint into the college quadrangle and disperse to the lecture rooms, the laboratories, the libraries and the dissecting room. They glow with exultation that they've done it again, in spite of their fears and natural disinclination to make fools of themselves, and at the same time sigh with relief that the ordeal is over for another week.

Stanley Browne is amongst them. Indeed, he is now the leader, for it has been discovered that he has a flair for open-air speaking and plenty of experience too, so who better to be the first to start preaching as they group themselves on the pavement outside the Gaiety, the ice-breaker so to speak, the one to catch the attention of the passers-by? And if one of the others falters and dries up sooner than expected, Browne can step into the gap and carry on the meeting as though nothing has happened. So it has become his weekly responsibility to keep the meeting going and every Friday he knows he won't be able to eat anything at lunch-time. 'I've got a sinking feeling in my epigastrium,' he confides to his companions. 'It's the thought of that open-air meeting, standing up and preaching to nothing! Let's go and pray about it first!' Like the others he dreads it but he dares it, and once he's on his feet preaching the fear goes. Often he stays behind to talk to someone who wants to ask questions, or to exchange a few remarks with the friendly policeman who has said with a wink, 'I'm here to uphold the law, but you young fellows are upholding grace. I'm a Christian, too. You go ahead and preach. I can't see that you're causing an obstruction!' And from time to time he can be seen standing with bowed head beside a passer-by who has paused to listen, and now wants to pray . . .

Right from the start of his college career Stanley became thoroughly integrated as a member of the small but very active Christian Union. On the Open Day at the beginning of college term he made straight for their stand to enrol, passing by the various other college societies touting for members. Sport, politics, art, drama . . . he was determined not to be deflected. 'Put God first,' his father had always said, and this was one way to do it. Link up straightaway with a Christian group intent on prayer, Bible study and propagating their faith. He knew what he wanted in the way of hearty, wholesome fellowship with those of his own age and outlook on life. He always asserted that his links with the Christian Union were the determining factor in his life at college and he had nothing but gratitude to God for the encouragement and the stimulus of the opportunities afforded through it at King's.

'We were a very lively union, with people from several faculties—arts, science, medicine, law, engineering. It was said that the C.U. was as lively as the Communists in advertising its meetings and trying to get converts. We took this as a tremendous tribute!'

When he had been a year at King's he was elected president of the C.U., so what with giving a lead in this, as well as continuing in the Christian Endeavour and Boys' Own at Drummond Road, his spare time was fully occupied, though he managed to play cricket and hockey to keep his body fit, and attend a weekly evening class in Latin.

It was during this year that the thought of becoming a medical missionary deepened into a settled conviction. His mother's death in hospital, and what he saw of the care and skilful treatment given to her there had impressed him, and he told one of his friends, 'I am determined to dedicate my life to the relief of suffering—and to discovering the *causes* of disease, and finding a cure.' Then he added, 'With God's help, I'll do it.' The question to which he had no immediate answer was how to get started on what must obviously be the full medical course. As well as attending a Greek class he had enrolled for the Intermediate B.Sc. course, taking physics, chemistry, botany and zoology, and at the end of the first year found himself in the top half-dozen in a class of sixty. Rather to his own surprise, he passed the Intermediate B.Sc. without difficulty.

What should be the next step? The more he prayed about his future career, the more his mind swung to medicine, and eventually he decided to approach the London County Council about it. So he gained an interview with officials in the Higher Education Department, showed them his examination results, and asked if they would be willing for him to transfer to the second M.B. course.

'A full medical course? But that means six years, and the Scholarship is only for two years.'

'Yes, I realise that.' Stanley explained that he wasn't asking for anything more from them, merely permission to use the non-vocational scholarship as a stepping-stone to a full vocational course.

The officials were sympathetic and extended his scholarship for a third year. As they said, it really did not matter to them what course he took, provided he knew there would be no more money coming from them for the last three years of his medical training.

'Thank you very much,' he said. 'I just wanted to know it would be all right to switch. I'll do my best.' He didn't know how he would be supported for the remaining three years, but the conviction that this was the path his Master intended him to take was so firmly rooted he knew he must take what appeared to be a risk. God had provided already in an unexpected way. He could do so again.

So he embarked on the medical course, and found to his surprise that his reputation in a quite non-medical sphere had gone before him. On his first day in the dissecting room he received a message that the Professor of Anatomy wanted to see him. Wondering what the interview would be about he went along as instructed, completely unprepared for the reception he was to receive.

'I've heard that you're a keen Christian,' said Professor Blair. 'And also that you've had experience in holding open-air meetings.' Stanley wondered what was coming, and waited rather uncertainly for the professor to continue. 'Now I've been asked by my church to conduct an open-air service next Sunday on the towpath at Richmond and I'd be glad if you could give me some advice and hints . . .'

Stanley expressed himself later as having been so flabbergasted that the proverbial feather was all that was needed to bowl him over altogether, but he managed to retain his equilibrium, regain his breath, protest his inadequacy, and then give the leading anatomist in the country the same instructions as he gave to the undergrads who joined the C.U. open-air team.

'Keep your head up—if you've got notes don't look at them. Speak clearly, but don't shout. Most important of all—*have something to say*. Your sincerity and the reality of your personal experience will shine through. Hesitancy and stumbling of speech will be forgiven but insincerity—No!'

'Thank you very much. Most helpful,' said the professor, jotting down a few notes. 'You can go now,' and Stanley backed respectfully out of the room. It was the beginning of a real friendship between the two.

Nor was it the only one he had with men much senior to himself. He had enrolled for the weekly lectures in theology held at King's for those who were not full-time Divinity students, but who wished to obtain the Associateship of King's College. Most of the lectures were given by the Dean, the Rev. Dr. W. R. Matthews (later to become Dean of St. Paul's), whose interpretations of the Scriptures did not always agree with those of the C.U. members. A group of these, Stanley included, sat together near the back, high up in the lecture theatre, nudging each other when the right reverend doctor came out with some pronouncement out of line with the evangelical tradition. At the end of one of his lectures in which he had been discussing the possibility of double references in orally transmitted tradition before the New Testament was written down he said,

'It's very obvious that the feeding of the multitudes was an example of a double oral tradition of a single event.' There was an uneasy stirring in the back row. 'Obviously there were differences, but these could not be of any importance.' He drew his lecture to a conclusion by asking if anyone had any question they would like to ask.

He little knew what he was in for. A slim figure in the back row shot to his feet and asked,

'In the matter of this double tradition, Mr. Dean, is it not possible that our Lord Himself had the idea that this would be a criticism in after days, and in order to spike the guns of those who would criticise He actually answered one of His disciples' questions in the following words,' and reading very clearly from his Bible Stanley continued,

' "Do ye not yet understand, neither remember the five

loaves of the five thousand, and how many baskets ye took up? Neither the seven loaves of the four thousand, and how many baskets ye took up?" '

There was a momentary silence, then followed an unexpected outburst of clapping and feet-stamping from the students in the theatre while the Dean, somewhat discomforted, admitted thoughtfully,

'Yes, I think you may have a point there.' It was the beginning of what became something of a feature at the end of the lectures—Browne courteously heckling the Dean, and the Dean equally courteously responding to the challenge. It was all very good-humoured, although each was on his mettle, defending the faith as he saw it, and a relation of mutual respect and even affection sprang up between the two of them. From time to time Stanley was in the Dean's room discussing the theological viewpoints on which they differed, the Dean eager to know what the students generally were thinking and saying about some of the controversial statements he made.

It is worthy of note that the persistent heckler passed the A.K.C. examination at the end of the first year with first-class honours, at the end of the second year obtained the prize given to the medical student taking the course who obtained the highest marks, and the next year obtained the Leathes Prize and also, on the strength of an essay on 'Evolution and the Problem of Evil', followed by an interview with the Dean himself, was awarded the Warneford Prize and Medal in divinity.

By this time he was getting a reputation for walking off with all the prizes although when, in March 1930, he took the second part of second M.B. and was runner-up for the University Gold Medal, he was amazed at his success. It was at this point he realised he had been, as he expressed it, 'entrusted with certain intellectual gifts which were to lead to God's glory and help other people'. In what particular way he did not know. His preaching, both in the pulpit on Sundays as well as in the open air, was having an obvious effect on individuals as one here, one there, turned in faith to Jesus Christ as Lord. To prepare himself for medical missionary work—that was what he was aiming at, and all his activities must be subservient to it. 'It all comes from God,' he said when people congratulated him on his successes. 'And it's all going back to Him, with His help.' It became a sort of stock phrase, and he fell back on it gratefully. It helped to remind him, even more than his friends, that he had nothing to boast about.

How he was to complete the last three years of his medical training he did not know. The ninety-pound grant each year had proved just adequate to meet his needs. When all other expenses were paid he had about a shilling a day for fares and food. Fortunately for him, a twopenny fare on a tram took him most of the way to and from New Cross, and he walked the rest. His midday meal, usually consisting of bread and cheese and apple was washed down with water. Almost unconsciously he was bringing his body into line with its needs, not necessarily its desires.

But the grant was running out, and he could not continue his studies unless money were forthcoming for another three years. Those weeks and months of 1930 were shadowed by the financial uncertainty. He prayed daily that God would make the necessary provision, and at the same time made enquiries as to any grants that might be available for impecunious medical students. Yes, there were two Baptist colleges that offered scholarships for medical students, and as a staunch Baptist he felt justified in making application. He had already got through the preliminaries when he received an official letter from the Higher Education Department of the L.C.C., asking to see him.

Unknown to him, others had been at work on his behalf. When he went for the interview, not knowing what it would lead to, he was asked,

'Are you still wanting to finish your medical course?'

'Yes,' replied Stanley without hesitation.

'Where is the money for the next three years coming from?'

'I don't know.'

The chairman fingered some papers before him, then looked up kindly.

'We have been very impressed by your college record,' he said. 'We have here recommendations from your tutors, and a letter from the Dean of King's College Hospital saying he will be more than willing to have you as a clinical student there. The Higher Education sub-committee has considered all these documents and would be very happy to give you a three-year scholarship at King's to cover your tuition fees . . . and ninety pounds a year for three years.'

And as he was also awarded a Raymond Gooch scholarship, he found himself at last free from acute financial anxiety, with three years' medical training ahead of him, and still able to live at home since King's College Hospital at Denmark Hill, south-east London, was within easy reach of New Cross.

There were plenty of people to rejoice with him, and he saw to it that all his friends knew of his good fortune. It was characteristic of him that he shared news like that.

There was one point, however, on which he had to admit failure, for almost the first time in his short but highly successful academic career. He had taken the primary F.R.C.S. course at King's College, and sat for the examination in June, 1930. He did not pass. The realisation that it was no unusual thing for students to fail that particular exam was small comfort to one who was accustomed not merely to passing, but to walking off with all the prizes. It was a somewhat subdued and crestfallen Stanley Browne who admitted at the church in Drummond Road that he had failed, although he had sufficient insight to be privately aware that it was probably rather good for him. 'Put me in my intellectual place, knocked the egotistical stuffing out!'

The news was received with dismay and sympathy by the members of the Boys' Own. 'Mr. Browne didn't pass the exam!' They were somewhat vague as to what exam it was, but one thing they knew was that it had cost him five pounds to enter for it. Five pounds! It was a lot of money, and who knew whether he could afford to have another try? Three of the older members got together and conferred about this aspect of the disappointment. Wasn't there something they could do to help him? 'Let's club together and send him the money. But we mustn't let him know where it's come from. Send it anonymously.'

So one day Stanley received an enveloped addressed to him in writing he did not recognise, and opening it pulled out five one pound notes and a letter which ran cryptically,

'We have been very impressed with your academic record. We have been feeling with you at your failure to get the primary F.R.C.S., and we should like to enclose the examination fee if you feel led of God to take the examination again. With our prayerful wishes.'

To those who did not know him well Stanley Browne appeared a cheerful and level-headed young man, not easily swayed by feelings. They did not discern the times when the rims of his eyes were suddenly tinged with red and moisture momentarily dimmed his vision because of something he had seen or heard. They would have expected him to pocket the money in his businesslike way, and since the gift had been sent anonymously and therefore could not be acknowledged, to destroy the letter. Certainly he pocketed the money and used it in the manner indicated a few months later, when he successfully passed the exam. As for the letter, however, he put it away rather reverently, among his private and personal papers. He did not know from whom it came, but it spoke of a love and a loyalty that touched his heart. Fifty years later it was still one of his most precious possessions.

*　　*　　*

The day came for him to go for the interview necessary to

determine his admission as a clinical student to the King's
College Hospital. He went along to be questioned by a rather
gruff, elderly ophthalmic surgeon who, with Stanley's college
record before him, chose to ignore his academic attainments
and snapped out, rather abruptly,

'What games do you play?'

If Stanley was taken aback by the question he did not
show it.

'Cricket, hockey, football, tennis,' he replied.

'What's your fielding position in cricket?' persisted his
interrogator.

'I both bowl and bat fairly well.'

Apparently his answers to those two questions were
satisfactory. He was not a bookworm who neglected
the physical needs of his body, who took no healthy
exercise. He was duly accepted, and enrolled as a clinical
student.

He sometimes said that the next three years passed like a
flash, and that he enjoyed every minute of them. He was
singularly free from strain during this period. The acute
financial stringency was passed, home life resumed its
smooth running again when his father remarried—Nellie
was a born home-maker—and the activities of the Christian
Union in hospital were as stimulating and encouraging as at
college. Again he found himself in demand as a speaker and
a leader in the group and, as at college, conducted a
missionary study group. He worked hard. The same studious
application was brought to the clinical aspects of medicine
as had been brought to the anatomy and physiology of the
pre-clinical course, and gained the same success. He came
to the end of the clinical course in 1933, with an impressive
list of prizes and honours to his credit—in obstetrics,
gynaecology, surgical pathology, hygiene and public health,
diseases of children, orthopaedic surgery, psychological
medicine, urology.

He had early decided to take the M.R.C.S. and L.R.C.P.
examinations because at that time it was possible to do them

in four parts.* Having passed them successfully, thus becoming a qualified doctor, M.R.C.S., L.R.C.P., he then took the whole London M.B., B.S. examination the following month. He was pressing himself hard, but he was confident he could do it. He had an aim in view.

When the time came for the results to be published, he went to the notice-board in South Kensington and looked eagerly for his name in the pass list. It was not there. It did not seem possible that he had failed, and he looked again. No, it was not there. He had been conscious of having done well, and could think of no reason for having failed.

Then he noticed a separate list. It was the honours division and his eyes ran quickly over the few names, coming to rest with great relief on his own. He had not failed after all! Not only had he passed with honours, but had gained distinctions in surgery and forensic medicine and hygiene.

By this time his plans for the future had crystallised and the course ahead was clear. From early childhood he had heard talks by members of the Baptist Missionary Society about work abroad, had studied the monthly magazine, had attended the annual meetings. While still at college he had approached the society about missionary work, and the needs and opportunities in a vast area by the Congo River had been put before him.

'The White Man's Grave' was a title still applied to equatorial Africa at that time, and the history of Protestant missionary work there was darkened by death after death of young workers who were cut down by disease within weeks of arrival. As for the children of missionaries, the death toll had been so alarming that it was now a rule that none should be brought up in the Congo. Even those born there should be taken home to England when their parents went on leave, and left behind in the care of relatives or friends. The risk

* M.R.C.S., L.R.C.P. This qualifying examination could be taken in four separate parts, and each part could be taken (and passed) at three-monthly intervals. It was considered as a kind of insurance against failing the final London M.B., B.S. examination.

of infection, once a child could run around and escape the protection of a clean house and garden was so great that it must be avoided even though it meant separation from parents at a very early age. There were already too many little graves in the cemetery in Stanleyville, or in quiet corners of mission compounds.

In the vast region known as the Belgian Congo the B.M.S. had opened five hospitals. One of them was situated in an area where, in addition to malaria and tuberculosis, intestinal disorders of numerous kinds and a score of tropical diseases, the tse-tse fly had brought the dreaded sleeping sickness to so many villages that it was estimated that thirty per cent of the population was affected. Yakusu, on the banks of the Congo some twelve miles downstream from Stanleyville, was the name of the village where the hospital had been built, and it had become famous largely through the genius of Dr. Clement Chesterman, the missionary doctor there. Not only had he brought sleeping sickness under control, but he had begun a programme of community health throughout the district, which was at that time unique. After giving some basic medical training to young Africans he had placed them in villages far and near on the river banks and deep in the tropical forests, to teach hygiene and practise simple medicine, while he and his colleague maintained oversight of them all by visiting them regularly and dealing with difficult cases. His wife, as enterprising in her way as he in his, had opened an elementary school in Yakusu itself, which had grown so rapidly that there were now five hundred pupils in it. This phenomenal advance in education and medicine had taken place among people only just emerging from cannibalism, and still under the deadening influence of the witch doctor. A large number, however, had embraced the Christian faith, and on all points missionary work centering in Yakusu was flourishing. The needs and the opportunities, it was asserted, were almost overwhelming. The small band of B.M.S. missionaries, stretched to its limit, was crying out for reinforcements, and the outstanding need was for a well-qualified young doctor who could eventually take the place of Dr. Chesterman himself.

Those were days when there was an underlying note of urgency in the evangelical world, bringing with it a strong pressure on young people whose sights were set on missionary work overseas. 'The time is short!' The cry was like a trumpet, and who shall say it was not prophetic, the rallying call to take advantage of the few brief years before the global conflict of the Second World War ushered in a more uneasy age? 'The evangelisation of the world in this generation.' 'To the work while it is still day! You have barely time to fulfil your commission!' Solemn warnings were given to beware of the strategy Satan could use to hinder those bent on carrying the Gospel to the regions beyond. The pull of family ties dimming the paramount claims of the One who said, 'Whoso loveth father or mother more than Me is not worthy of Me'; the lure of human love leading to early marriage and settling down; the temptation to gain higher and higher distinctions in one's chosen career until earthly advancement loomed larger than heavenly gain, and the mission field was ruled out.

The subject was frequently discussed in the hospital Christian Union, where interest in missionary work was keen. All these legitimate affections and ambitions could become snares to trap the unwary. Stanley, as President, was conscious that his own actions would influence others and was determined at all costs to get to the Congo as soon as possible, and not be deflected. Yet there was still so much to be done. He must put in a year in hospital as house physician, and more months in Belgium for the study of French and tropical diseases before he could set off for that hospital in Yakusu. Two years at the very least, and even then he would have had the minimum of experience in both medicine and surgery! Well, a step at a time!

He applied for what was the most coveted house job at King's College Hospital, that of house physician to the Senior Consultant Physician, Sir Charlton Briscoe, and obtained it. On his first night on duty he was called to

the Casualty Department. A colleague of his, a personal
friend in the C.U., was casualty officer, and wanted his help.
A man who had attempted suicide had been brought in,
obviously requiring something more than medical treatment.
'He's in real spiritual need, Stanley. We must help him!'
They gave him the medical treatment he needed, but they
didn't leave him then. They listened as he talked—then they
talked and he listened.

'Jesus Christ . . . He can give you the inner strength you
need. Jesus Christ . . . He can help you. Ask Him into your
life. Ask Him to take you on. He'll do it. He's promised
never to turn away anyone who comes to Him.'

So the man believed what the two young doctors told him,
and before he went to sleep that night he had acted on their
advice. 'Lord Jesus, come into my life . . .'

They looked into each other's eyes as they stood by his
bed, the two young men in their white coats, and were silent
for a moment. It was the first night for both of them to be
in charge, a milestone in their medical experience. They
knew each other well, they knew each other's aims. 'I started
my training with the conviction I should be a medical
missionary,' Stanley had asserted, while the other, equally
convinced, had said, 'I want to be a surgeon and serve the
Lord in Government service.' They had come thus far
together, and now this had happened.

'On our very first night—a soul led to Christ! It's the
Lord. He's set His seal on our being here.'

*   *   *

Stanley Browne's medical career was being watched by
some of the eminent men at King's with a closer interest
than he realised, especially by those who knew and sym-
pathised with his determination to become a medical missionary. Among these was Mr. C. P. G. Wakeley the senior
surgeon at King's, and perhaps the best-known surgeon in
the country. He was later knighted and became President of
the Royal College of Surgeons of England. 'The Admiral',

as he was respectfully referred to behind his back (he had been Rear-Admiral at Haslar Hospital in Portsmouth during the 1914–18 war), was a strong Calvinist. While many of his colleagues had little time for the Christian Union members who were unlikely to become general practitioners ready to send them their well-to-do patients for consultations in Harley Street, he was eager to encourage them. So one day Stanley, having completed his six months as house physician, done a locum as Medical Registrar, taken the Membership examination of the Royal College of Physicians of London, and obtained the Murchison Scholarship as the most outstanding graduate in medicine for the last two years, on a visit to King's was called by the Dean into his office in the medical school.

Stanley had come to somewhat of a standstill by this time, and was uncertain as to his next step. His application for a house surgeon's job at the Royal Northern Hospital had met with a cool reception. Meanwhile, the urge towards the Congo was increasing. He wanted to do six months as house surgeon as soon as possible, and then move on, although he knew he would be unlikely to get as wide an experience in so short a time as he felt he needed.

But God had a plan, and had His agent ready. It was at this point that Mr. C. P. G. Wakeley opened for Stanley the door which was to provide him with all the experience any young surgeon could hope to cram into six months. He invited Stanley Browne to apply to his firm at King's as senior House Surgeon.

This was the gist of what the Dean had to say, and Stanley, realising he was being offered the job all the budding surgeons at King's regarded as the best, could scarcely believe it to be true.

'But I've already had the plum house physician's job at King's!' he exclaimed. 'That's why I didn't apply for a house surgeon's job there.'

'Well, you've got the opportunity now. Mr. Wakeley has intimated he'd like you to apply. I advise you to do so.'

The next six months were the most strenuous and exacting Stanley had ever known. At one time Mr. Wakeley's firm had twenty-three private patients scattered about the hospital, twenty-four 'acute beds' in two wards, and sick children in another. The house surgeon's nights were sometimes hectic. Stanley was rarely in bed before midnight and often called after that by anxious night sisters worried about their patients. It was during this period he cultivated the ability to drop into a sound sleep within a minute or two of closing his eyes.

But the experience he gained was outstanding. He was allowed to do about ninety major operations himself during this period of six months, with the help of sympathetic senior colleagues. 'Browne, you do this,' one of them said as they scrubbed up together before dealing with a particularly nasty appendix. 'You might get something like this when you're on your own in the Congo or somewhere!'

They were stimulating days, though shot through with conflicting ideas as to his own immediate future. Should he join the Baptist Missionary Society and set off for the field as soon as he had finished his house surgeon's job, or should he remain in Britain for further training and experience, as some were advising?

'No one should open the peritoneum who can't deal with what they're likely to find—including a volvulus! You won't be able to phone for your "chief " or get the aid of another registrar when you're in the wilds of Africa!' urged one school of thought.

'But many promising young doctors have been lost to the mission field altogether through getting so involved in surgery they've eventually settled at home. If you wait till you're equipped to meet every emergency, you'll never go!' was the equally emphatic argument on the other side.

He was the object of more prayers during that period than he ever realised, and perhaps that explains why, in the end, the two apparently conflicting viewpoints merged. He took the final examination for the F.R.C.S. and also the

Master of Surgery examination of London University in mid-1935 and failed both. He had been accepted as a candidate for B.M.S. by this time, and went to Antwerp for the study of French and tropical medicine. His knowledge of French was already so good that he could follow the courses without any difficulty. In addition to coaching fellow missionary students less fluent in the language he revised his surgical work in preparation for re-sitting the F.R.C.S. in December. This time he was successful, and a few weeks later obtained the Diploma in Tropical Medicine in Antwerp.

His former fellow-students at King's gasped when they heard it. 'Browne! He's F.R.C.S. and M.R.C.P., and he's just got the Diploma of Tropical Medicine in French. And now he's going to the Congo!'

The press got hold of the news, too. Not only did the local papers and the Christian periodicals come out with glowing reports of the former Brockley boy who had become a 'famous surgeon', but he made headline news in the national press.

'HE WENT TO A LONDON COUNCIL SCHOOL—SCHOLARSHIP PATH TO DISTINCTION', was blazoned in the London Evening News, and Sunday papers followed suit with 'ELEMENTARY SCHOOLBOY BECOMES DOCTOR'.

'It is a case of a man reaching the heights from a very humble beginning,' a friend of his at King's told a reporter. 'He is a very modest, unassuming chap, and never makes much of his achievements.'

Whatever may have been his natural sense of gratification at this fanfare of publicity, it had its embarrassments for one who was now a member of the medical profession. It might be construed by some as being a form of self-advertisement, to have got in the papers like this. A few days later, therefore, a little paragraph was inserted in the British Medical Journal under the heading 'Disclaimers'.

Mr. S. G. Browne, F.R.C.S. (London, S.E.14) writes:

My attention has been drawn to several paragraphs which have appeared in the press recently, giving highly coloured accounts of my career. I presume that the facts were drawn from an official report of a public body whose scholarship I held as a student. The inferences must be the result of journalistic imagination, since neither I nor the members of my family have at any time given interviews to pressmen.

Somebody has suggested that missionary work, like most worth-while callings, consists of ninety per cent perspiration and ten per cent inspiration . . . Owing to an oversight I was left stranded by a river bank without means of conveyance, and had to wait some time for a lorry to take me a further stage on my journey. I judge that I had already expended my ninety per cent of perspiration since five o'clock that morning. Meanwhile, I heard the drum calling the children of the village to school. I went along, and was soon in the midst of a crowd of laughing black faces. We learned a new hymn about the way to the Heavenly City, and then I told them about some of the difficulties on the way, illustrating my straggling remarks by reference to an experience the previous day when the *camionnette* in which I was travelling failed to mount an extremely muddy incline and slid, with effortless ease, into a ditch at the side of the road. The mud was well over the axles, and it took the united strength of all the able-bodied men in the nearest village to extricate it. 'Our sins are like the mud on the road: they hinder us in our journey to the Heavenly City.' Some time later, when we were able to recommence our journey, I felt curiously light of heart, happy to have had the opportunity of casting seed into hearts apparently receptive. That was my ten per cent inspiration that day.

S.G.B.
Yakusu
April 1937

CHAPTER FOUR

In the Belgian Congo

Those who believe that God has a plan in life for His servants can see, on reflection, how they have been prepared for its fulfilment by occurrences that at the time seem merely incidental. When a young Honours graduate in history taking her teacher training at Oxford attended a memorial service in the Bloomsbury Central Baptist church in London, she went along mainly because it was being held to honour the memory of Dr. Fletcher Moorshead, a personal friend of her family. She sat up in the gallery, with a friend who had been at school with her in China where she had spent her childhood, looking down on the platform and feeling rather solemn. She knew several of the people on the platform, though there was one she had not seen before. Young, slight, taking his seat rather diffidently, he did not attract her attention until the chairman announced:

'Mr. Stanley Browne . . . the last of the medical students Dr. Moorshead saw through missionary candidate training . . . shortly to join the B.M.S. team in Yakusu, in the Belgian Congo.'

As she was interested in missionary work in Africa, though without any idea she would ever go there herself, she listened with quickened attention to the tribute now being paid. Then, 'What a marvellous speaker!' she whispered to her companion. There was something about the young man's restrained eloquence that moved her deeply. She did not see him again for five years, but she did not forget him.

In the case of Stanley, the apparently incidental occurrence that was to prepare him for his destined pathway was a course of lectures on leprosy at the Antwerp School of Tropical Medicine. They were delivered in a particularly animated and fascinating manner by a Belgian leprologist, and richly illustrated with micro-photographs of histological damage and clinical photographs. Stanley's imagination was fired.

'Professor Albert Dubois was in touch with most people working in leprosy; he was familiar with the old German work that emphasised the importance of the nasal mucosa as a portal of exit of leprosy bacilli; he realised the importance of damage to peripheral nerves by cellular infiltration and oedema; and he stressed the interest of leprosy as a worthy scientific pursuit of immense social importance. He was convinced that the disease was very widespread throughout the Belgian Congo,' he wrote. He had learned a little about *Mycobacterium leprae* and the peripheral nerve damage of leprosy in the course of his medical studies, but never before had he met anyone with so wide and so fervent an interest in the disease.

Up to that time medical concern about leprosy had been mainly confined to the compassionate efforts to alleviate the suffering of its victims by a few missionaries, Roman Catholic and Protestant, in various parts of the world. However, the International Leprosy Association had been created in 1931 and since then some steps had been taken to elucidate some of the many puzzles surrounding the disease. Men like Robert Cochrane and Ernest Muir were doing their best to stir up scientific interest in the subject, and a big International Leprosy Congress was being planned, to be held in Cairo in 1938. Meanwhile chaulmoogra oil and its derivatives provided the only known means of arresting the disease, and their effectiveness was limited to its milder forms. Nothing could be done for the people with lepromatous leprosy. They were doomed.

It was in Antwerp that Stanley Browne saw, for the first time, some leprosy sufferers. They had all caught the disease in the Belgian Congo—planters, nuns and priests and a bank clerk. There was no expectation of a cure for them. The best they could hope for was that with good food, good living conditions and medical oversight the extreme ravages of the disease would be held at bay.

What he had learned about it theoretically took on a new dimension when he saw it in reality, but it did not occur to him then that this was the beginning for him of what was to become a deep, almost total commitment to the cause of leprosy. As far as the work ahead of him was concerned, he expected that surgery would claim much of his time when at the base in Yakusu, and community health generally, with the control of sleeping sickness in particular, when on tour in the district. He had been given an outline of what his duties would entail, and a general idea of the sort of diseases he was likely to meet with. Leprosy was listed along with impetigo, and pustular infections of the skin, onchocerciasis and various kinds of mycoses. And as skin diseases were only one aspect of the medical problems, like intestinal parasites, and as malaria was rife, and all the sorts of conditions that result from malnutrition, to say nothing of the after-effects of the witch-doctor's ministrations, added to the normal disorders and accidents to which the flesh is prone the world over, he had no idea of specialising in anything. Rather, he would have to do the best he could at everything.

And so, in April 1936, he set off at last for the Congo, ten years after he had sat for the London Metriculation Examination which set him, a mere junior clerk in the Town Hall at Deptford, on the road to medical school. The long period of preparation was behind him at last, and a lifetime of missionary service in Africa, as he expected, lay ahead.

The journey took him again to Antwerp, giving him the opportunity to say goodbye to the kindly Belgian woman who had been his landlady while he was staying there. He had a special affection for her, and she for him. It was during his stay in her home in the rue van Dijck, and through his encouraging her to read the Bible for herself to find out what it said, that she had become a believer in the One Who can claim, 'No man cometh unto the Father but by me.'

'It was a tremendous thrill for her to realise that she could now worship God through Christ alone and read the Bible which she had scarcely seen before . . . had regarded it as a wicked Protestant book,' wrote Stanley. She was quite outspoken, and prepared to assert her faith in the face of priestly argument and opposition. For Stanley her clear conversion was the crowning joy of his very satisfying time in Antwerp. He made no secret of his conviction that in the long run souls are more important than bodies.

The journey to the Congo was by Belgian liner to the port of Matadi, and thence by train to Leopoldville (Kinshasa) the capital, where he parted from his four travelling companions, new missionaries like himself. He never saw them again. Within two years three of the four were dead, a grim reminder of the price paid in those days to carry the Gospel to equatorial Africa.

Stanley was required by Belgian colonial law to do a *stage pratique*, working under supervision in a government hospital and laboratory before he was permitted to practise in the Belgian Congo. The customary month was reduced to a fortnight in his case, but it gave him the opportunity to get acquainted with Belgian officials and medical men with whom and under whom he would afterwards be working. Then the time came at last for him to proceed to Yakusu, a thousand miles farther inland on the upper reaches of the Congo.

He travelled by plane, an unusual experience for a missionary in those days, and got an awe-inspiring aerial view of the vast forests that rolled like a green ocean to the horizon, dotted here and there with neat plantations and straggly villages. The quiet security of the fields and hedges, the hamlets and lanes of rural England seemed very far away. This engulfing green ocean threatened to submerge all the little clearings that man had made in it. Only beside the great river snaking its way through the territory had humanity managed to establish itself, clinging to the banks tenaciously in towns and villages. As he approached Stanleyville he scanned the river bank below eagerly, just making out what he was looking for as the plane slowly dropped to a lower altitude—the two-storey building alongside a collection of corrugated iron roofs that was the Baptist Mission compound at Yakusu.

The plane glided on through the air, then taxied to a halt in the airfield at Stanleyville. A bearded veteran Baptist missionary with an old Ford car was there to meet him, and a six-foot-three giant of a man who introduced himself as Dr. Raymond Holmes. So this was to be his senior colleague in the hospital! He had come to meet him and escort him to Yakusu.

At the riverside Stanley was plunged with bewildering suddenness into his new life in Africa. Standing beside a long slender dug-out canoe, waiting for him, were twelve stalwart dark-skinned men, naked from the waist up, richly tattooed all over, each holding a twelve-foot long paddle as though it were a spear. They shouted loudly as they saw him approaching, and started to advance in what appeared a threatening manner, paddles held as though they were spears.

Stanley, somewhat bewildered, tried not to look alarmed. 'It's all right,' Holmes assured him. 'They're just telling you they're glad to see you. It's their way of welcoming the new *Bonganga*, the new white doctor.' '*Kelekele*!' he called out to the men. '*Kelekele*! The *Bonganga* thanks you!' They boarded the canoe, the paddles were plunged into the water with a triumphant whoop, and off they set.

It was an impressive twelve-mile journey downstream to Yakusu. As they approached each little village on the banks of the great river the drums throbbed out the news of the new *Bonganga*'s arrival and smiling Africans poured out of their huts to wave and shout a welcome. At the Yakusu landing-stage a guard of honour composed of smart young medical trainees was headed by the pastor of the church who, thirty years before, had been a cannibal. The bank was lined with hundreds of white-clad children from the Mission's schools, and crowds of people swarmed behind them, eager to catch a glimpse of the new *Bonganga*. At the top of the steps leading up from the jetty stood the whole contingent of Baptist missionaries, eighteen of them, looking with interest at this new colleague. From a predominantly African scene below he found himself walking along a road that might have been a stretch of English seaside promenade, with a row of neat bungalows facing a grassy sward, ending abruptly in a steep cliff over the swift-flowing brown waters of the Congo.

At the last bungalow, the one nearest to the hospital, Raymond Holmes turned and leading the way in showed Stanley his room. 'Sorry it's so small, Browne,' he said. 'But it's all we've got. We'll get some shelves put up for your books, and anything else you need to make you comfortable. Meanwhile, we'll have to hurry. The Millmans have invited us to their place for dinner tonight at seven.'

There was no time to put his things in order, still less time for reflection. Hastily Stanley stripped and washed, changed into a clean suit and brushed his hair. The grinding noise of cicadas and crickets dinned in his ears, moths, flies and midges whirred around his head, but underneath it all one word glowed in his mind.

'Browne! He dropped the Dr. and just called me Browne!' Those were the days when forms of address were punctiliously observed, and titles were only dropped between friends and equals. That this tall, friendly man, his senior in age as well as position in the Mission, as soon as they were alone together, should so simply, so naturally have spoken to him as one who was an equal, accepting him without reserve as a colleague and a friend, warmed his heart. It was the beginning of a partnership of mutual affection and confidence which rode out all the possible storms when views on medical policy might differ. Stanley's academic qualifications, exceptional for a young man not yet thirty, far exceeded those of Raymond Holmes, yet Holmes was the doctor in charge. The situation was one fraught with the possibilities of tension and resentment. Stanley's natural gifts along other lines, his fluency in French, his musical accomplishments (with a little tuition from his sister Winifred he had learned to play the piano quite well), his preaching ability, could have made it even more difficult for the older man. But the fact is that the two of them worked together in Yakusu for twelve years 'with very little friction', to quote Dr. Holmes, who added, 'It was perhaps the happiest period of my life.' It was also the longest medical association in the history of the Mission.

All this, however, was in the future, though on that very first night Stanley got another glimpse of the calibre of the man with whom he would be working. They were at dinner together in the Millman's house, the gleaming white table-cloth artistically decorated with crimson flowers, and delicious food served by smiling African schoolgirls providing an unexpected introduction to missionary life, when a commotion on the verandah outside was followed by the appearance of a panting, sweating man who had jumped off his bicycle and was standing at the open door.

'S'il vous plaît!' he gasped, and held out a letter. It was for Dr. Holmes who tore it open immediately. It was an urgent plea for help. The manager of a coffee plantation and factory down-river had been taken suddenly and seriously ill. Holmes took it quite calmly. It was evident that there was no conflict in his mind as to what he would do. He would go. There was no question about it.

'I'll have to leave about two a.m. to get there by dawn, he said. 'Better get three or four hours' sleep if I can.' The journey ahead involved travelling by the Mission's river launch for forty kilometres, then on his motor-bike over rough dirt roads for another forty. He looked across at Stanley, and said with a wry smile,

'Dr. Browne, I must leave you in charge of the hospital. Sorry you haven't had a chance to see over it yet, but you've met Sister Moyles at the quay—she'll show you around. It's Sunday tomorrow, so that means only routine work—providing there aren't any emergencies . . .'

Inevitably, there were emergencies. Stanley was called early next morning to a young woman in the throes of impacted labour. Picking his way across sleeping bodies sprawling on the beds, under the beds and beside the beds, he was led to a small side ward in which three women, in addition to the hospital nurse, were trying to comfort the moaning girl he had come to see.

'Can't you get some of these people to go outside?' he whispered to the nurse, but she shook her head.

'They're her mother and her mother-in-law and the local midwife,' she explained in a low voice. 'Better let them all stay. They're used to having their own people with them. It makes them feel more secure.'

So that explained the overcrowded wards. Not all those recumbent bodies were patients. The majority were their relatives, who had come to keep them company and cook their meals for them. He soon became accustomed to having an interested audience whenever he examined a patient. Even the operating theatre had its peep-holes and relatives looked in through the windows at what was going on.

Although outward conditions were so different, the routine of his life at Yakusu fitted into a pattern quite similar to what he had been used to at home, for it mainly revolved around his patients, the hospital and his desk. Shortly after five-thirty a.m. the drums sounded, and at six a.m. he and Raymond Holmes went for the roll-call of the twenty-odd *infirmiers* with their shining dark faces and clean white uniforms, the young men who were being trained in simple medicine and hygiene. A short worship service with them, then on to the roll-call of the workmen, and the daily distribution of rations for patients and staff from the hospital stores. If there were no patients urgently requiring attention, breakfast was the next item of the daily programme—'Better make it a good one! You never know when you'll get your next meal!' Then came the busy life of the medical missionary with the ward rounds and the out-patient clinics, the operations and the emergencies, the preaching sessions and the private interviews, the supervision of the compound workmen and the training of the *infirmiers*, the medical auxiliaries.

The training of these medical auxiliaries soon became Stanley's main charge. 'You've got a flair for teaching, Browne,' said Holmes. 'You've had experience, coaching those students at King's up to their finals, and I know you're interested in it. So I'd like you to take on the Senior *Infirmiers'* classes. Your French is well up to it. Do your very best with them!'

It was an appointment that would have far-reaching consequences, for on the young *infirmiers* depended the manning of the medical outposts over the vast area of ten thousand square miles for which the B.M.S. had been given responsibility.

The history of that Rural Medical Service, already known as a model in tropical Africa, had its roots in the First World War, when young Lieutenant Mathewson of Dunfermline was killed in Belgium in 1918. His family, in memory of him, contributed a sum of money with which the Baptist Missionary Society proposed to start a medical mission in Yakusu, near Stanleyville in the Belgian Congo. The Mayor and Mayoress of Plymouth undertook the support of the first doctor. A little dispensary had been run there for some years, but now a hospital was to be built and a doctor installed.

That is how Dr. Clement Chesterman eventually got there, fresh from military service in Gallipoli and Palestine where he had ridden a weary horse surely if somewhat slowly into Damascus, to be involved in the horrors later so graphically depicted in the film, 'Lawrence of Arabia'.

The significant thing about that spectacular and bloody victory on the plain of Megiddo was that more died from malaria and influenza than from the weapons of war.

Chesterman was recommended for the O.B.E., not for prowess on the battlefield but as a result of his activities against the unseen enemy that had proved more deadly than the Turkish army. The little laboratory for which he was responsible in Damascus was run in shifts of sixteen hours each day while he went around the hospitals collecting blood smears. He was there in time to diagnose hundreds of cases of malaria just at the end of the incubation period—and cure the victims. An ardent admirer of Dr. David Livingstone, he said later, 'It was malaria which killed Mrs. Mary Livingstone on the Shiré River in 1855, and ruined the health of the doctor after his porters had absconded with his supply of quinine. I was glad to be able to fight this million murdering malaria . . . !'

On his arrival in the Belgian Congo late in 1920, he was recruited into a war against another microscopic murderer. This time it was sleeping sickness, which was known to have killed three hundred thousand people in Uganda at the turn of the century, and was now decimating vast areas around Stanleyville. Miss Louise Pearce of the Rockefeller Foundation had discovered what promised to be an effective remedy for the disease—tryparsamide—and the Belgian colonial authorities were eager to put it into use. They politely inferred that they were not interested in British Baptists who wanted to open a hospital in which to perform operations on local people. The British Baptists could open the hospital if they liked—after all, Britain and Belgium had been allies in the Great War—but they must expect no help from the Government for that. If, on the other hand, the British Baptists were prepared to co-operate in this fight against sleeping sickness they would have the Government behind them, ready to give them every reasonable assistance. They could go where they liked, preach what they liked, so long as they waged war against the *Trypanosoma gambiense*. The land was before them, ten thousand square miles of it. Into the plantations for rubber, the plantations for coffee, the plantations for any and everything they could enter freely, on that condition. Fight sleeping sickness!

Dr. Clement Chesterman, late Lieutenant of the Royal Army Medical Corps, accepted the conditions. The hospital was built in Yakusu and equipped to meet local needs for curative medicine and surgery. It also became the training ground for the auxiliary medical workers who were put in charge of the clinics he established, one by one, in the plantations and villages around. To them he went with the famous needle that had already proved so effective as a weapon against yaws, and which now began the fight against sleeping sickness. The potions and incantations of the witch doctors proved no match for the needle of the white doctor, whose fame spread far and wide as the dreaded disease was gradually brought under control. But the rural clinics continued and increased in number, as other diseases were diagnosed and dealt with, for as Dr. Chesterman said, 'Congo was a paradise for parasites. There were four forms of malaria, two trypanosomes, four filariae, five common intestinal worms, three varieties of bilharzia; smallpox, meningitis in epidemics and endemic leprosy everywhere affecting from two to fifty-five per cent of the population . . .'

That Community Health Service from Yakusu on the banks of the Congo was probably the first of its kind in the history of modern medical missions. The hospital itself was officially recognised as one of the two teaching hospitals in the Belgian Congo by the time Stanley Browne joined its staff. He had entered into a rich inheritance, and his admiration deepened, not only for the man who had laid the foundation of this steadily expanding work, but also for Raymond Holmes who had backed him up for the last few years.

There was a good spirit among the missionary team, and for Stanley the pleasantest hour of the day was the period before the evening meal when, having washed and changed, they all gathered on the grassy sward on the cliff overlooking the river, relaxing after the day's work and chatting together in the comparative cool of the early evening.

They always changed for dinner, and the men were punctilious in the way they behaved towards their wives. 'It may seem silly to observe such formality here,' Holmes explained to Stanley, 'But we hope we shall be imitated eventually. So far even our most civilised African boys don't eat with their wives. They just take their meals in comfort, being waited on, and the women take the leavings.'

Many were the meals Stanley took alone, however, for the claims of the medical work pulled him and Holmes in different directions. For days, sometimes weeks on end, Holmes would be away visiting the outlying dispensaries, while Stanley would be left in charge of the hospital and the school. As he walked back to the bungalow at the end of a busy day he savoured to the full the vivid contrasts of life in Africa. The charm of the fireflies flickering in little clouds under the trees. The irritation of winged insects, small, large, quick, cumbersome, brushing his face, or if one of the sudden tempestuous tropical storms whipped up, the rain like spears beating down on him as he ran for cover. The croaking of frogs, the grinding sound of the cicadas, the hooting of owls and jackals and hyenas, always a background of sound that sometimes seemed so deafening he had to shout to hear himself speaking. There might be a romantic silence of the African night to be enjoyed in other parts, but not here by the Congo.

Back in the bungalow that was spartan in its simplicity, lacking so many of the conveniences and comforts of homes in England, it seemed ludicrous to change into a clean suit, sit down to a carefully-laid table, and be waited on by a smart young African, eager to please. He hadn't been accustomed to household servants, but here everyone employed them to do the washing, the carrying of water, the cooking over a simple, wood-burning stove. There was great competition to get a job in a white man's house, for that meant free schooling and lodging, food and new suits of clothes. 'Keep a sharp eye over all your things—they'll be pilfered if you're not careful,' he was warned. He hadn't been accustomed to that, either, or having to lock everything up and keep his key in his pocket. Nor was he used to having the electricity cut off at nine-thirty p.m. and having to finish his desk-work by the light of a hurricane lamp.

The contrasts in personal living, however, were slight compared with those he soon became aware of in life all around him. The huge Mission compound with its well-swept paths and its orderly programme was like an oasis of civilisation among the sprawling villages along the river bank. The neatly dressed African schoolchildren and the trim young *infirmiers* who lived on the compound, responding alertly to the drums that summoned them to their classes, seemed to belong to a different world from the lethargic, ill-nourished, poorly-clothed villagers.

It was the malnutrition and the disease among the rural Africans, with their tropical ulcers and yaws and distended stomachs that impressed him. He came in close contact with them in the hospital and saw how much of their suffering was due to ignorance of the simplest rules of hygiene, and of their superstitious fears, nurtured and preyed upon as they were by the witch doctors. The shrieks and wails of a young woman who arrived at the hospital one day, clad only in a strip of printed cotton around her hips, were due not to any physical pain but to her conviction that she had been bewitched. She had found some chicken bones and blood strewn outside her hut, a sure sign, she said, that she had been bewitched and was going to die before sunset.

Stanley observed with interest that once she had been calmed down and reassured she quickly dropped off into a peaceful sleep, and the sedatives he had been going to prescribe were not necessary. The African, he soon learned, did by nature that which he had deliberately trained himself to do in his busy houseman's job at King's, snatching rest when he could and falling asleep within a minute of head touching pillow.

When fierce emotions were aroused, however, it was surprising how long the African could keep awake, as he discovered one night in a rather alarming manner. It all came about over the death of a sixteen-year-old girl during a difficult labour with her first child. Her relatives were strangely indifferent to her condition, their attitude being 'If she can't give birth to her own baby, she doesn't deserve to live.' However, when she died, and the baby was delivered by a rapid Caesarian section, it was a different matter. Their dark faces peered in through the window of the operating theatre, watching proceedings, and when they saw the living child they took not the slightest notice of it. They spent the rest of the night wailing loudly, until as dawn broke the death wail rose to a crescendo. Stanley, who had not had much sleep himself, went to the window and saw a crowd of Africans, many of them with bodies bedaubed with chalk and wearing necklaces of leopards' teeth, armed with long spears, advancing in a menacing way towards the hospital. They were out for his blood, it seemed, asserting that he had killed the girl and that they would kill him. The senior missionary, who had dealt with this sort of situation before, succeeded in quietening them, but not in persuading them to take the baby. There was evidently some sort of deep-seated taboo where the child was concerned and not even the grandmother, the usual one to come forward in such circumstances, would have anything to do with it. The family eventually dispersed sullenly, leaving the baby behind for the missionaries to look after.

When Raymond Holmes returned from his tour in the district and heard what had happened he acted wisely. It was good for young missionaries to be introduced as gently as possible to the real Africa. It was better that Stanley should first have had a taste of what he might encounter alone in the bush while he was still in the comparative security of the Mission compound. 'It's all experience,' he said. 'You've had plenty of it in the hospital—I'd like you to start taking your turn in the district now. There's a missionary who's sick down-river at Yalemba. Go and see her, bring her back here if necessary, then go on to the lower Topoke. It'll be a new district, and I want you to open it up. Make a medical census of the people in the villages. There are about thirty-six villages I think. We'll send Lotoba with you. There have been twenty-three cases of sleeping sickness reported, but that's not all you'll find.

'Leprosy is one of the biggest problems now. Very widespread. Chesterman reported it to the authorities, but they discouraged him from doing anything about it. It's not a killer, after all. That was their retort. Concentrate on sleeping sickness! Leave leprosy alone!'

And there was no cure for the insidious, mysterious, creeping disease anyway. They already had their hands full dealing with the killers—the malaria, the sleeping sickness, the smallpox, the tuberculosis. But it would be good if they could have a leprosarium to take in the bad cases, care for them a bit . . .

'What happens to the bad cases?' Stanley asked.

Holmes slowly shook his head. 'Don't know. Never been able to find out. No one talks about it.'

There was so much to be done, the days were so full, there was no time for speculation or investigation. As far as Stanley was concerned, in addition to the medical and teaching work and taking his turn with preaching, he had to apply his mind to learning the Lokele language. Having to plunge straight into a full-time working programme meant that language study must be fitted into odd moments. The whole question of leprosy had to be shelved.

When questions were shelved in Stanley's brain, however, they were not forgotten. They were there, neatly tabulated and indexed, ready to be produced promptly when the right time came. And when they were produced, he did something about them.

I have just returned from a rather sad mission. Consequent upon a State decision, part of the territory for which we have been medically responsible for the past year or two has had to be ceded to another authority, and it was my unpleasant task to go and close the central dispensary serving the area.

When we began to pack up the bottles of drugs and mixtures various, and the scales and measuring flasks, the paramount chief who was looking on realised that we were actually withdrawing from the work, and his disappointment knew no bounds. At first he was angry and inclined to accuse us of wilfully leaving him and his people in the lurch. However, I spoke to him as follows;

'You have many wives, but if I were to take one of them away from you by force, you would feel sorrow in your heart. I have to look after people of many districts, but if one district is taken from my care, do I not also feel sorrow in my heart?' He appreciated the force and cogency of this argument. The chief then dilated on their love for and trust in, the *infirmier*. Not till then did I fully realise the extent to which this boy had endeared himself to these wild folk, caring for them in their sicknesses, and helping them nearer God. It was rather pathetic to see an old woman clasp him round the waist, and cry, 'But he mustn't leave us.' Had my mind harboured any lingering doubts concerning the value of our rural medical work as an evangelistic agency, these doubts would have been dispelled as morning mists before the rising sun.

S.G.B.
Yakusu, 1938

CHAPTER FIVE

A practice the size of Wales

He looked very incongruous, clad in a white coat right there in the middle of the forest, sitting at a little folding table with a cloth on it, peering into a microscope. A few scraggy chickens were pecking at the rough ground, a snarling scavenger dog cowered near by, and a group of tribesmen in loin cloths stood watching him uneasily. The *Bonganga* had examined them all, listened to their heartbeats through the long tube thing he hung around his neck, pricked their skin with the tiniest of needles, and with the utmost care, as though they were priceless, smeared the drops of blood that appeared onto a piece of glass. And now it was apparently one of those specks of blood he was looking at through the pipe that had glass at the end of it. It was all a very strange sort of magic, very quiet, too, with no rolling of drums or beating of breasts, whirling of skirts or brandishing of spears. Uncanny. They preferred the gesticulations of the witch-doctor, his cries to the spirits, his leaps into the air, fearsome though might be the consequences of his invocations. His antics at least had the virtue of being familiar, the sort of thing they were accustomed to. But this strange silence and intense application, this use of weird instruments, this writing of signs on paper, all allied to the man with the pale skin and light eyes that seemed to see something you hadn't known was there, and the quiet voice that spoke some words you knew and some that you didn't—it was all rather ominous and made you suspicious of what lay behind it.

However, there was no doubt about the remarkable power

79

of the needle he wielded. Almost before their very eyes the raspberry-like lumps on their bodies and the bodies of their children, the horrible yaws, had disappeared after *Bonganga*'s needle had been thrust into their arms or their buttocks. They'd lived with yaws for years and now, after only two or three pricks of *Bonganga*'s needle, their skin was smooth and clear and free from those oozy lumps. No wonder everyone was clamouring for the needle. If it could cure yaws in a matter of days, surely it would clear up malaria too, and put a stop to aches in the stomach and pain in the chest.

And his medicine! The worms it could produce after one dose, a whole jar full of them, you'd never have believed so many could hide themselves in one small child's belly! And his knife! There were a lot of mysterious preliminaries connected with that knife, much boiling of water and lighting of lamps, much wasteful use of good white cloth and swabbing of flesh, but once the *Bonganga* had the knife in his hand it was remarkable how quickly and quietly he plunged it into the flesh, and how soon the hard lump was cut out and there was no more pain.

And it was all done with a silent concentration, followed by a lift of the head and a brief word of command to Lotoba, then a turning to the next person waiting in the line to be attended to. The dwellers of the lower Topoke forest had never seen the like of it, and they were intrigued, mystified, pleased yet apprehensive. They'd heard about the white man with the needle, but this was the first one who had come to them. They stared and stared.

Conscious of the curiosity he was arousing, Stanley looked up with what he hoped was a reassuring smile. This was missionary work as he had pictured it, here in the heart of equatorial Africa, with himself the only white man among thousands of dark-skinned, tattooed tribesmen of the forest. Just so must David Livingstone have sat outside his hut less than a hundred years ago, trying with the limited means at his disposal to alleviate their sufferings. Just so, more recently, had Clement Chesterman sat, as he battled on their behalf with sleeping sickness. And now he, Stanley Browne, was continuing the fight against the diseases that ravaged them. This was the culmination of those years of preparation back home in England, this was the life to which he had been called. There were times in the midst of the toil of travelling and the hardships of living when an ineffable joy flooded his heart as he sensed the presence of the One Who had promised, 'I am with you always.' Not for anything would he have changed places with the most eminent consultant in Harley Street!

He was taking his full share of the district work now, out on trips lasting from two to six weeks, making a medical survey. Raymond Holmes had allocated a new area to him, the lower Topoke forest, where a few teacher evangelists had been placed in some of the larger villages but where no doctor had yet visited.

Those teacher evangelists won his affection and his admiration as he saw the conditions in which they lived, and compared them with those they had become accustomed to in Yakusu. He had seen them back there in Yakusu, rows of beaming, shiny-faced young men in the classrooms, trim and upright in their clean shirts and shorts, disciplined, healthy, tidy, laughing together on the sports ground, praying together in the church, earnest in their decision to serve their Master wherever He should lead them. Now he saw them in a different setting—the straggling, untidy villages with heaps of filthy refuse, unwashed bodies and dark superstitious ceremonies, the dreary background in which the neatness of their own little huts and the well-swept paths around the rough building that did duty for school and church, stood out in sharp contrast. These young men had received sufficient education to widen their horizons, give them the delight of mental achievements, and now here they were, scattered far apart and living amongst people whose experience was bounded by what they knew of the silent forest and their fears of the unknown. He felt for them in their loneliness, knew what his visits meant to them as they opened their Bibles by the light of a hurricane lamp when the day was over, and prayed together. And when one or another of them failed and left his post in shame, as sometimes happened, he knew in some measure the grief of the shepherd who has lost one of his flock.

In some of the villages he visited, however, there was no teacher evangelist, and he tried to preach, in his stumbling Lokele, to the people who gathered round to watch him bake his bread and eat his evening meal. He got accustomed to the stern routine of each day, rising early to knead dough, put it on top of his food box where it could gently rise during the day, setting off on his bicycle with his fifteen-year-old houseboy and Lotoba to visit the villages. The flies, the mosquitoes, the sticky heat, the narrow slippery paths, the swamps into which he slipped occasionally, the fallen trees over which he must carry his bike, the perpetual green twilight of the forest. Then the arrival in a village, greetings exchanged with the chief, the lining up of all the villagers, the setting up of the table with the medicine chest and the simple laboratory equipment, and down to work.

'I began the early examination of villages in a very naïve, Western-orientated fashion, listing people under the diseases they were suffering from, but I soon abandoned this method. They were all suffering from various skin diseases, various kinds of mycoses, impetigo and pustular infections, leprosy . . . They all had malaria, more or less chronic. They all had at least two intestinal parasites. So we considered this as read when examining the villagers and concentrated on the more unusual conditions. This was an area which until then had had no medical treatment at all, and where malnutrition was rife. It introduced me to the struggle they had in order just to exist.'

The scientific interest in leprosy generated in him during those lectures in Antwerp prompted him to observe closely the skin manifestations of the disease which he frequently saw, and to study the different causes of loss of pigment.

Only occasionally did he see someone with a clawed hand or an ulcerated foot, evidence of neglected leprosy, but very few in the advanced stages of the disease. Why?

He asked the village chiefs. So much leprosy—where are the people who had been blinded by it, whose feet and fingers had ulcerated away? There must be some like that. Why hadn't they come forward to be medically examined like everyone else?

The chiefs shook their heads. 'There are none in this village,' they said.

'Where are they then?' The chiefs shrugged their shoulders. 'None here.'

Then came the day when he saw them, the unforgettable day when he rode suddenly into the clearing and saw those low huts out of which crawled human beings like worms out of the ground, stretching out ulcerated maggoty hands . . .

He was a doctor, accustomed to decay, but he had never seen anything like this. The stench alone made him retch.

It wasn't only the physical distress that broke in upon his consciousness like a flood, though. It was their eyes, human eyes out of which stared desperate, despairing souls. Eyes in which there was shame, that inexplicable sense of shame that accompanies leprosy. Beings from whom others shrank away. Outcasts.

In a way he could never explain, what he saw that day was something beyond that tiny colony of hopeless leprosy victims dying in an African forest. It was the foul disease itself, and the web into which it was enmeshing its victims, millions of them, all over the world.

'And this was really the beginning of my deep spiritual and medical commitment to leprosy. I promised there and then, not only to do what I could to help them, but to prevent other people becoming like them.'

*   *   *

The experiences in life which pierce the deepest are often those we are the most reluctant or unable to divulge. Stanley

Browne was a good correspondent, having a natural fluency of expression in writing which, allied to his businesslike methods of dealing promptly with matters requiring attention (in addition to everything else he wrote about fifty letters in French each month), meant that even during his first term of missionary service he not infrequently appeared in print. At least three contributions from him appeared in the *British Medical Journal* and the *Nursing Times*, in addition to letters or articles published in the Christian press and King's College Hospital magazine. He reported some medical cases, reminisced about valiant pioneers of the past, told of daily life at Yakusu and the opening of the new church building. He wrote vivid descriptions of the scenery and the people, their tattooed bodies and their living conditions. He took his readers on his journeys by boat and bike, showed them the mud-baked crocodiles basking in the sun, the leopard prowling round his hut at night, the deadly snake that missed him by inches, the confrontation with a witch-doctor who was eventually arrested by the village chief and marched defiantly off to jail after having changed into a European dinner-jacket, white trousers and shoes. He introduced them to some of the Congolese Christians whose lives had impressed him, and expressed his satisfaction in the life he was living.

'While pushing a pen in an office I never imagined that God would call me to be His witness as a doctor in the heart of Africa, and I am more than thankful when I look back on the way in which He led. There have been far too many coincidences to doubt that God is in it all,' he wrote early in 1937.

But of the human horror he had seen on that particular journey into the forest he wrote nothing. Not until many years had passed did he realise it was perhaps the most significant 'coincidence' of all, for his itineraries never took him there again. He only saw that rotting decay of the living once, but it had shed a glaring light on all he had learned about leprosy.

He told Raymond Holmes of it, however, for Holmes,

too, was concerned about the prevalence of the disease, and from time to time, along with other members of the Mission they had talked of the need for segregation and the possibility of opening a leprosarium for that purpose. They could not hope to cure the sufferers—only provide a shelter and some medical assistance for them when needed. The important thing was to get the infectious cases where they would not pass on the disease to others, and tentative dialogues were already going on with the Belgian medical authorities about camps for that purpose. As Stanley and Holmes were only together for about ten days at a time between their itinerations in the district, however, there was little opportunity to press forward with vaguely formulated plans. Then something happened which delayed them further, and forced on Holmes one of the most painful choices of his life. An urgent cable from England informed him that his wife was seriously ill, and that he ought to return to be with her.

To go immediately would mean leaving Stanley Browne, only six months out from home, in sole charge of the medical work. Already the medical staff had been drastically reduced by the unexpected recall of Dr. Chesterman, earlier in the year, to take up an important mission appointment at home. It had meant throwing Browne in at the deep end and he'd done splendidly, but he'd had practically no opportunity, usually accorded to new missionaries, for language study, and his knowledge of Lokele was still defective. At the very last choir practice he had led in the church he'd announced that they would now sing, 'While shepherds cooked their flocks by night'. It had raised a laugh at the time, but Holmes had realised the difficulties under which his young colleague was still labouring. How could he leave him just at the time when, in addition to everything else, the annual accounts and reports had to be completed and the *infirmiers'* exams were coming up? It was more than one man could carry, and would retard the whole work.

On the other hand, there was Nora. They had been married less than four years and already she had suffered so much with the death of their first baby whose little body lay in a tiny grave under the trees in the European graveyard. When she knew she was to have a second child they had both agreed she should return to England for the confinement. Her health was already impaired, and they could not face the possibility of losing another little one. The separation had been hard, but it had been worth it. Only a few weeks ago the news had reached him that he was the father of a healthy little son, and the mother was doing well.

And now this cable! The decision he came to on his knees before God that day was made just a little easier because he knew his wife.

'I'm not going yet. There is too much work here,' he told Stanley, adding quietly, 'Nora will understand . . .

'I'll stay until the reports are done and the examinations over, and a relief is on the way.' *Nora will understand.* Stanley got a glimpse that day of the depth of the unity that could exist between husband and wife, a unity that could transcend the strain of separation. It was moving, and inspiring.

Not until several weeks had passed, and the news came that a young doctor from New Zealand, Trevor Knights, was preparing to come to Yakusu did Raymond Holmes leave his post to return to England—and the death-bed of his wife.

'We shall all miss him terribly while he is on furlough,' wrote Stanley in an unusually self-revealing letter home. 'While we were feeling rather depressed, and wondering how all the acute problems now facing us would be resolved during the weeks when only one doctor would be on the station, we held our usual weekly prayer meeting for the hospital staff. "Usual" did I say? But it was far from ordinary. As one and another of the *infirmiers* and *infirmières* rose to thank God for the life and witness of the doctor who had that day passed by Yakusu homeward bound, and as we prayed for the constant blessing of God upon him and his, our hearts were strangely moved, and we felt that our cup of inspiration was full to overflowing.'

Six weeks were to elapse before Trevor Knights was due to arrive, and during that time Stanley gave the hospital staff a bad fright by crashing through the ceiling of the operating theatre and landing on the cement floor below with a thud. He had been up in the roof finding out why the electric lights had fused when the ant-ridden beam on which he was poised gave way. Blood was oozing from his wrists which had been torn by wires as he fell, and cries of '*Asowa! Asowa!* He is dead!' rent the air. Rather to his own amusement later on he realised that his own flashing thought as he crashed to the ground was a somewhat irritated, 'Now I've killed myself, and the new doctor hasn't got here yet!'

Little damage was done, as it happened, but a few days later he developed acute dysentery, and that proved more serious. He was in bed with a high temperature when Trevor Knights arrived, and he had to hand over responsibility to the newcomer, doing his best to help him with instructions and explanations from his bed. But when he was told that one of the patients had a mastoid requiring an immediate operation, he knew his must be the hands to perform it. It was the first mastoid case they had had at Yakusu. He couldn't let this young doctor, just out from home, tackle a job like that. Why, they hadn't even got all the instruments that would be required! In defiance of his knowledge that he ought to stay in bed he got up, thinking rapidly. A surgical hammer for chipping the bone. There wasn't one, so what?

'Go to the carpenter's shop and bring the smallest hammer he's got there, and boil it with the rest of the instruments,' he instructed Lotoba.

Two hours later, just as that operation had been successfully performed, another crisis arose. The wife of one of the *infirmiers* had a serious internal haemorrhage, and while she was being prepared for an emergency operation a man was brought in who had been attacked by his mother-in-law and had to have his wounds stitched. Then back to the *infirmier's* young wife in the operating theatre. He had just made the incision when, to his horror, he realised that her heart had stopped beating. What could he do? Quick as a flash his hand went in through the incision and he began to squeeze the heart rhythmically. To his intense relief it began to beat spontaneously.

What with one thing and another, by the time he got back to bed again Stanley was too exhausted to realise that he seemed to have skipped the convalescent period.

Things settled down after that. Trevor Knights proved to be a very adaptable young man, as well as a very reliable medical colleague. He was soon taking his share of the district visits, enabling Stanley to continue not only the routine work of the hospital, but that which stirred his enthusiasm, more than anything else—the training of the *infirmiers*.

It was in those classes with the *infirmiers* that, quite unconsciously, he prepared the network by which he was to gain his practical experience in the widespread prevention and treatment of leprosy. In its way it was a fascinating study, and just as the professor in Antwerp had captured his attention, now he proceeded to attract the attention of these eager young African students to it. This baffling disease of leprosy was a challenge that medical science must not ignore! In time they would be going to take charge of dispensaries in the forests, on the plantations, along the river banks, and on them would largely depend the health of the local communities. What a responsibility! And what an opportunity! They would be able to observe at first hand diseases which research workers in laboratories could only study through microscopes and the perusal of other people's findings. They would be able to see what the disease did to the person, see the effect of it on the whole man, not just its effect on the tissues of his body.

'Observe!' He remembered how Mr. Wakeley at King's had used that word time and time again in his lectures to the young medical students, and how he had followed it up. '*Think* about what you see. Then record it.'

'Record!' The keeping of accurate records—so much

depended on this. Not only on account of the treatment of the individual patient, but also in the cause of medicine world-wide could those records be of vital importance. Discoveries were often made through the painstaking perusal of meticulously kept records, and when those discoveries were made, when some conclusion was arrived at that could throw fresh light on the subject, then it must be shared. It was criminal to withhold medical knowledge which could help to combat disease and alleviate suffering. One of the primary functions of medical journals was to share information.

'Publish!' Those three words, observe, record, publish, were deeply imbedded in his own mind, and he impressed them on his listeners. They were involved in something far greater than they had realised, their observations and records could help forward the universal fight against the diseases that dogged mankind. The inspiration of it gripped them, and they were ready to co-operate. The making of notes and keeping of accurate records on the cases they dealt with and the diseases they saw should be an integral part of their medical work. '. . . including leprosy. Even though the only thing that can be done so far is to give these painful injections of chaulmoogra oil, that don't do very much good. But keep records! Keep records!'

His interest in the progress of the *infirmiers* continued after they had been sent to their various assignments. He started writing to them, an activity that eventually led to the establishment of a correspondence course, and he was just as eager to see them on his medical itineraries as the patients they had gathered for him.

Not all his patients were villagers in the backwoods, however. The B.M.S. doctors also acted as general practitioners for the scattered whites in the population, and organised a medical service for all the Company workmen and their families. The whites paid liberally for these services, providing the hospital with its largest source of income. Without the fees they paid it would have been impossible to provide so thorough and extensive a medical service as was given at nominal rates to the Africans.

This G.P. service to the whites often accounted for the emergency calls to which the doctors responded, and it was when Stanley was returning from one of these that he arrived late one day at the river to find, with dismay, that the hospital launch was not where he had left it. His eyes scanned the serried ranks of canoes moored along the bank in vain— the launch was not there.

'Where's the *Limengo*?' he demanded sharply of the crowd of bystanders. It could not have been stolen. It was too well known for anyone to make off with it successfully, and in any case there were too many people around.

'The other *Bonganga* took it. Here's a letter for you,' was the reply, and a note was thrust into his hand. He tore it open and read,

'I have been taken ill and am returning to Yakusu. Very glad of *Limengo*, sending it back for you. Trevor.'

The writing was weak and straggly, and gave no indication of the nature of the illness, but Stanley knew it must be serious for Trevor to have abandoned the medical itinerary which was to have kept him in the bush for another two or three weeks. He had not long to wait to know how alarming it was. The motor launch returned at midnight, and with it a note from Nurse Moyles urging him to come as quickly as possible. Dr. Knights appeared to have tetanus.

The story of this case was of sufficiently dramatic and medically interesting a character to provide material for a page in the *British Medical Journal* later on. Trevor Knights, out in the bush, aware of unusual weariness after a twenty-eight-mile non-stop bicycle ride, took a drink, when suddenly his jaws went into spasm. He remembered the patient who had died two months previously in the hospital. It was tetanus that had killed him. He remembered some of the facts he had learned about the disease. Alone in that isolated rest-house he commenced his fight for life.

'Hurriedly altering notes I had written to various native

chiefs and colleagues about my future plans I completed the inspection of the dispensary, had a short sleep on the table and changed my clothes, sodden with perspiration at the unsuccessful efforts to take a meal, and rode back twenty-eight miles through a tropical downpour to the river bank.'

While waiting for paddlers for the canoe that would take him on the two-day journey back to Yakusu he looked up some medical notes and found that according to them his condition only left him about four days of very painful life . . . He decided that all he would take with him in the canoe should be his papers and a few drugs. Better travel as light as possible. He could leave the rest of his kit behind. He wouldn't be needing it again.

The providential appearance of the *Limengo* moored by the river bank cut his nightmare journey short by a day, so that twenty-eight hours after setting out on the trip that he thought would be his last, he was once more lying in a decent bed receiving expert nursing care. But the fight had only just begun. Stanley arrived back at five a.m. on the following morning, and for the next ten days he and young Nurse Moyles, also in her first term of missionary service, kept unremitting watch by the bedside of their colleague. His jaws were tightly clenched so that only with difficulty could the tube through which liquids flowed be inserted. The violent spasms that wracked him threw his head back so that his body formed a sort of arc as though being bent by relentless, invisible hands.

By the ninth day the illness showed a clinical picture of increasing seriousness and the patient's agony was wringing screams of pain through those clenched jaws. That night Stanley gave him 70,000 units of anti-tetanic serum intravenously, and 9,000 units intramuscularly, and watched through the long hours. Morphine seemed to have no effect, and Trevor had begged not to be given an anaesthetic.

There was a tense, living stillness over the whole compound. 'Oh, God, spare him!'

The next morning came the most violent contraction of

all. It was as though those relentless invisible hands were squeezing the life out of his body, and when it was over the pulse was imperceptible and the respiration ceased for two minutes.

'He'll never survive another,' thought Stanley rather desperately. He saw the expression on Nurse Moyles's face. If Trevor had another spasm it would be death to something in her, too.

But Trevor did not have another spasm. Instead, miraculously, he slept. And when he awoke, he himself knew he was going to live.

*　　*　　*

Weeks passed before he recovered completely however, and some months later, after his marriage to Nurse Moyles, he was transferred to another hospital. Once more Stanley was single-handed, and with all the routine work of the hospital and district to attend to, in addition to training the *infirmiers* and taking his turn in preaching, the thought of leprosy again had to be shelved. There was no opportunity for him to turn his attention to it effectively. The right time had not yet come.

Things were astir elsewhere about which, in the full and exacting life of a medical missionary in a neglected area, he knew little or nothing. A Congress on Leprosy, convened by the International Leprosy Association, was being planned to be held in Cairo early in 1939, just about the time Raymond Holmes, having made arrangements for his little motherless child to be cared for, was due to return to Yakusu, so it was decided he should attend the Congress first, as a delegate of the B.M.S.

Although he himself was not present, that Conference proved to be of strategic importance in Stanley's life. It was one of the largest ever yet held, with three hundred delegates from fifty-five different countries. After that, leprosy was officially on the medical map in the Belgian Congo at last. Sleeping sickness had been almost entirely stamped out, and now the Government was prepared to do something about leprosy. Surveys were to be made to discover the prevalence of the disease throughout the country, and to the *docteurs anglais* at Yakusu was entrusted the task of undertaking one in the 10,000-square-mile district for which they were responsible.

Raymond Holmes and Stanley saw in this the way towards eventually realising their ambition to open a leprosarium with official backing. The first step was to make the survey.

'I think you're the one to do it, Browne,' said Holmes as they discussed it together. 'You've already gone over the district several times, and you've got this interest in the disease. Take some of the *infirmiers* in training with you. It will be experience for them, and relieve you of some of the routine work.'

And so Stanley, nearing the end of his first three-year term of missionary service, went off to obtain what proved to be the best opportunity he could have got anywhere in the world to observe leprosy in its various forms in the early stages.

'The method was to go for a four, five or six weeks' journey into one of the *chefferies* of the district and then, with the *infirmier* in charge of the local dispensary, we called the population of the villages together, primarily for sleeping sickness control, but in addition to register all the diseases from which the population was suffering, with special concentration on leprosy. After the initial screening by some of the medical auxiliaries in training, I would see all those suspected of having some kind of skin condition or some disease of the peripheral nerves that might be leprosy.

'It was here that I built up my knowledge of early leprosy.' And his tutors were two ex-cannibals, one a witch-doctor, the other a village chief!

The value of his visits to these remote villages where his medical skill had alleviated so much suffering was evident now. The people knew him, and the men of influence, the chiefs and even some of the witch-doctors, were prepared to help him. They were far quicker than he to discern the early

93

stages of leprosy. What he had only learned from books they knew from personal observation, and as he sat, the chief on one side and the witch-doctor on the other, they would draw his attention to it.

'Look here, *Bonganga*. This is it! Turn round,' they would instruct the patient, then quickly they would point to a place on his skin where the slanting rays of the sun showed up something Stanley had not noticed. 'See the difference in the colour here? It's shiny—see? And there's a little sweating, too, on this one. Look!' Then they would murmur in an aside, 'That's the beginning of it. That's the mother of the bad leprosy.'

The bad leprosy. Early lepromatous leprosy the books called it, that which would eventually be disseminated throughout the body and destroy all the peripheral nerves. The bad leprosy these half-naked dwellers in the forest called it, and theirs was the more intuitive description when they saw that early, scarcely discernible gleam in the skin. 'There's the mother of the bad leprosy!' The village chiefs and the witch-doctors taught him what even the expert in Antwerp had been unable to convey.

'This then was early lepromatous leprosy, and this is how I learned about it. We went from village to village calling everybody together, and as a matter of fact we saw one hundred and ten per cent of the population! That is to say, we saw far more people than were officially registered for tax purposes with the Government and when we disclosed the figures we had seen village by village to the local administrative authorities they would scarcely believe us.'

The administrative authorities were readier to accept the facts placed before them than were the medical authorities, though. When Stanley reported that in the *chefferie* Kombe nearly half the population had diagnosable leprosy, the Director of the Belgian Red Cross and the Fonds Père Damien organisation refused to believe it. There could not possibly be so many cases in one area, he asserted. Stanley stuck to evidence and insisted that there were. In the end the Director, with commendable diligence, travelled from Stanleyville to accompany him to Kombe and see for himself what the real situation was, and at last he was convinced. 'This must be the highest prevalence rate of leprosy in the whole world!' he exclaimed.

And indeed it was. Stanley had found it.

. . . Be sure you are where God wants you to be. Often we have to choose between the good and the better, and the choice is not easy. 'He that findeth his life shall lose it, and he that loseth his life for my sake shall find it,' and these words are just as true today as when the Master first uttered them. If only we could see everything in the light of eternity and of God's will for us, the choice would not be as difficult as it sometimes is. 'Go up higher, may mean: accept a lower salary, or do a job less in the public eye, or carry out a thankless task. God's ways are not our ways.

I remember when my chief—a distinguished London surgeon—asked me to be his first assistant. I replied saying that I felt God wanted me to serve him as a missionary of the Gospel in another land. I don't for one moment regret that decision, because I realise it was God's will for me. Some of us may have to choose between the good and the better, and God's will for us is always the best.

I heard recently of a successful businessman who last year paid over six thousand pounds in income tax; he looked back wistfully and most regretfully upon the glowing faith he once had. . . . He might say with Disraeli, 'Youth is a mistake; manhood a failure; old age a regret.'

Be sure you are where God wants you to be, and you will not be accumulating for yourself in after years a whole memory-load of regrets.

S.G.B.
(Speaking in Westminster
Chapel, London, 3 May 1945)

There will come times of doubt, especially when work is dull and dreary and disappointing, and when success is withheld or delayed; you will wonder if God ever meant you to be a missionary, or if He intended you to work for Him in your present sphere or under your present auspices. You must not be dependent on apparent success for your spiritual health. If you are where God wants you to be, and remain in constant communion with Him, then your call will be frequently confirmed.

S.G.B.
1947.
*(First published by IVF in an article
called 'The Missionary and His
Environment')*

CHAPTER SIX

Love at first sight

The Rev. Dr. H. R. Williamson sat amongst the books and files in his London office, thinking. This job of being the Baptist Missionary Society's General Foreign Secretary was very different from what he'd been accustomed to in China for thirty years and more. He missed the clear blue skies of north China, the surging crowds in the markets, the coolies jogging along with their laden carrying-poles, the grave-faced, intelligent students, the inherent dignity of these people of an ancient race. On the whole he'd have preferred to stay among them had it not been for the girls. For their sakes he and his wife had been glad to accept the appointment that kept them in England where they could make a home for their three daughters, and it was of Mali, the eldest of them, he was thinking now. Unlike her two sisters, both of whom were progressing normally towards the married state with suitable young men of their own choice, Mali was still without any masculine attachment. Her interest in missionary work had always been deep, and her mother and he had secretly hoped that, like them, she would follow that calling. So far however, beyond accepting the position of missionary secretary in the Baptist church they attended, she had made no positive move, and seemed fairly settled in her life as a teacher.

Settled—yet not settled. This wasn't the life for which she had been born. As her father, he felt sure of that. It was more as though she were poised, waiting for a call, ready to respond when it came.

His mind switched to the coming interview with this

young missionary on furlough due to return in a month's time to the flourishing medical work in Yakusu, Dr. Stanley Browne. He'd made quite a stir on this, his first furlough, with press notices referring to him as a 'brilliant young medical evangelist', and 'one of the most brilliant medical men ever on the staff of the B.M.S.'. Even before he had arrived home there had been so many requests for him as a speaker that contrary to usual Mission procedure he had been plunged into deputation work almost from the start, with very little time for a holiday. His talk at the missionary meeting during the Keswick Convention had been outstanding, with its vivid picture of the spiritual effectiveness of the young *infirmiers* evangelists he had been training.

'Nothing but the best in the Master's service!' he had said. 'It's not good enough to dispense good theology and bad medicine. Our greatest contribution in the Congo is to train and equip African lads to carry the Gospel—and the blessings of modern medicine.' He had carried this message of disseminating truth and health through the painstaking teaching of others, backed by personal reminiscences vividly related, up and down the country, and interest in the B.M.S. work in the Congo had been quickened as a result.

Along other lines, too, in his contacts with some of the medical men who were eminent in their particular fields, it was evident he was making his mark. Altogether, Stanley Browne was a very promising and spiritually-minded young missionary, utterly dedicated, the sort of man to whom a father would confidently entrust his daughter. And he was still unmarried, evidently unattached . . .

So at the end of the interview which had dealt mainly with practical matters such as financing Yakusu projects, the policies to be adopted, and the manner of travel back to the Congo now that England was at war, Dr. Williamson said casually,

'By the way, you haven't visited our home yet, and I know my wife would like to meet you. We always enjoy entertaining our missionaries home on furlough, but you've been so booked up we haven't had the opportunity yet. Are you free next Saturday? If so, would you care to come to lunch and spend the afternoon with us?'

Stanley thought rapidly. An invitation to lunch from a senior official in one's missionary society was not exactly in the nature of a royal command, but all the same it couldn't be dismissed lightly. By a little rearrangement of his plans he realised he could fit in a visit to Sutton, which wasn't too far from New Cross anyway. It seemed the right thing to do.

'Thank you very much,' he said. 'I'd like to come.'

'I'll meet you at the station,' said Dr. Williamson, and after shaking hands Stanley departed.

He was nearly at the end of his first furlough, and not without a measure of heaviness was preparing to return to Yakusu. It had been good to be at home again, back in the heart of his own family, renewing friendships and making new ones. He'd been received with acclamation as Brockley's most brilliant old boy, his advent had been announced in the local press with the headlines 'They Beat the Drums When He's Coming', and of course the Drummond Road Baptists and especially the Boys' Own had all turned up to welcome him. The busy deputation programme, with its constant travelling, had continued even after the war with Germany was declared, and a 'Black Out' at night was imposed. He realised he had gone down well as a speaker, especially with young people. That questionnaire he had used, half-laughingly, to discover their fitness for missionary work had attracted a lot of attention, demonstrating as it did in an unusual way the sort of conditions he had endured in the Congo.

1. What would you do if your houseboy spoilt the only flour for making your bread when you were on trek 120 miles from your station?
2. Can you walk the tightrope? If so, could you cross a stream balancing on a tree trunk thrown across to span it, carrying your bicycle?

3. How would you regard the presence of snakes, tarantula spiders, lizards, hornets and driver ants in the little mud rest-house you were to occupy for the night?

And all along there had been opportunities for talks on spiritual matters with individuals eager for a closer walk with God. 'Never forget the early morning tryst with God,' he'd said to one. 'Take time to find God's will for your life,' to another. He'd spoken simply, out of his own experience, glad that he could do so.

The months had passed quickly, for in addition to normal deputation gatherings he had had a number of meetings with people in the medical profession. To some of them he had shown the microscopic slides he had made of scrapings from the nose and nasal mucus which had been painstakingly taken from suspected leprosy sufferers. His findings on this subject had met with doubting comments.

'These can't be leprosy bacilli—they must be contaminants,' was the general consensus of opinion, and even discussion with Dr. Robert Cochrane, son of the founder of the famous Peking Medical College, had had its disappointing aspect. Dr. Cochrane, acknowledged to be one of the foremost leprologists in the world, was as uncompromisingly evangelical as Stanley himself. 'Our work is to demonstrate, *within the context of the Gospel*, how disease in general and leprosy in particular can be controlled,' was his contention. For him the proclamation of a crucified and risen Lord was the missionary's primary commission.

Stanley was in complete agreement. To him those little gatherings when he had preached to the forest dwellers or the patients in the hospital with his Bible in his hand were as important as the physical examinations followed by the dispensing of medicines he had given them.

'And what we do must be well done. Slovenly work is a discredit to our Master,' was another of Dr. Cochrane's tenets, firmly re-echoed by Stanley himself. Stanley's colleagues, African and missionary alike, were to find his standards of absolute integrity hard to live up to at times. *Infirmiers* whose reports were proved inaccurate found themselves discomfited by an unsmiling silence, and a pair of steely grey eyes before which their own dropped in shame. He had little sympathy with those who were content with second-best.

That Dr. Cochrane did not accept his figures regarding the high prevalence of leprosy in the *chefferie* Kombe of the Belgian Congo was disappointing, but it did not lessen his respect for the man. 'Nearly half the population! This is impossible!' Dr. Cochrane had said. 'No place in the world can have more than ten per cent of leprosy. The only way to prove that these are leprosy germs would be to scrape the nasal mucosa and then fix and stain these preparations. If you find germs in clumps they must be leprosy germs and cannot be anything else.'

The pathologists and microbiologists he had seen had said that, too, and he resolved that when he got back to Yakusu he would institute complete microscopic examinations of all in his area who were suspected of having leprosy.

It was a mammoth task he had set himself, but it was not this that was causing the indefinable heaviness of spirit assailing him as he began preparing for his return to the Congo. He could rise to the challenge of the work, the hours he would have to spend at his desk studying and classifying the reports, the strain and discomfort of those arduous journeys into the forest. He was prepared for the discipline of mind and body that the life demanded. From his boyhood days in the Christian Endeavour he had schooled himself to endure hardship as a good soldier of Jesus Christ, and it was almost second nature to him now. None of those things could deter him. What was not so easy to accept, what was clouding his sky, was simply the loneliness to which he was returning.

Lonely. He hadn't been conscious of it in the first year or two at Yakusu, when the novelty of it all and the satisfaction of actually being a medical missionary in Africa had been sufficient. He had observed with the tolerant amusement of a friendly onlooker the development of the romance between Trevor Knights and Nurse Moyles as she helped to nurse him back to health, had aided and abetted them in it. He had not in the least begrudged them their happiness, but it had served to accentuate his own solitary state, and as time went on he had looked forward with increasing longing to being with his own family again. The knowledge that furlough lay ahead had been as the light of dawn over the horizon of his last months in Yakusu, mainly because it would take him back into the intimacy of the home at New Cross. No sense of loneliness there! But now furlough was nearly over, and it was back again to the 'Box-and-Cox' sort of existence he and Raymond Holmes shared in 'the doctor's house' as their bungalow was called.

Even if Winifred joined the team at Yakusu it would not make very much difference. He had been warm in his encouragement when she told him she believed God was leading her into missionary service, delighted that his own sister would be following him to the Congo. But he knew she would be living in the nurses' home, not with him, if she were designated to Yakusu, and that they would both be so busy they would have little time to spend together.

In any case, he would still have those tours of the district to do alone, days and weeks on end in the silent forest, with only the young African *infirmiers* for company. He enjoyed being with them, and had learned to enter into their lives—but how could they enter into his? With experience of little beyond Yakusu and their own villages, with no books, no magazines, no newspapers, no music, what did they know of the wider world from which he came? The mental isolation of those hours cycling through the forests was perhaps the dreariest prospect of all. Yes, it was the loneliness of his lot that weighed on him, the natural desire for what he saw others were enjoying—a happy married life.

'Stanley—you ought to get a wife!' he had often been told

and his answer had always been the same. 'Too busy to think about it!' And it had been true. All through those years as a clerk at Deptford, a student at King's, a young medico in hospital, a missionary candidate in training and then as a doctor in the Congo he had attempted and achieved so much, ever embarking on fresh courses and undertaking new responsibilities, that he had left himself no time to cultivate the sort of friendship that would lead to matrimony.

It was not that he had decided to remain single all his life. He had expected that eventually he would marry and have a family like other men, that somewhere along the line he'd meet a girl who would make him a suitable wife. But in that spring of 1940 he was becoming aware that such a thing might not happen after all. He was already thirty-two, within a month would be returning to a life of such a limited social character that the chances of meeting a girl he could love were extremely thin, and by the time he was back in England again he'd be almost in the category of being a confirmed bachelor. Was that God's plan for him? A monk-like existence? It was an unwelcome prospect, but perhaps it must be faced.

One weekend, when he was in Thanet as a convention speaker, a free afternoon gave him the opportunity to go for a long, solitary walk. During those hours he plumbed fresh depths of personal dedication as he faced up to what it would mean to go through life alone. He thought of those long silent journeys through the forests with no human being with whom he could converse on an equal level, and with no one of his own to return to when the trip was over. He thought of the bleak little room lined with book-shelves which was bedroom and office and study combined in the doctor's house—his home at Yakusu.

The temptation to turn away from it all was suddenly very strong. Not without a sharp inward battle did he get to the point where he could say sincerely, 'All right, Lord. If that is Your way for me, I accept it.' But he got there. It was not even his compassion for the people in those forests and along the banks of the great Congo river who needed so urgently the medical and spiritual healing he could bring them that brought him to that point, but the remembrance of his Master. His Master had known a loneliness far deeper than anything he would ever know. Jesus Christ had entered fully into the lives of men, but how could they enter into His life, His thoughts, He Who had come from the glory of eternity?

To go back alone to the Congo was a very small renunciation compared with that. Maybe it would prove to be, in some slight way, a sharing of His sufferings . . .

By the time Stanley got back from that walk the matter was settled as far as he was concerned. He was prepared to remain single for life, a doctor in Yakusu, and he expected that was how it would be.

It was in that frame of mind that he went to Sutton one Saturday late in March, to be met at the station by Dr. Williamson, who led him out to the waiting car and introduced him to its occupants.

'My wife . . .

'My daughter, Marion. But she's always called Mali. That's the way the Chinese pronounce her name.' She was wearing a big picture hat, and smiled at him in a friendly way. He'd met her once before, he remembered, outside the church. A beautiful girl . . .

They all went for a drive to Burgh Heath after lunch, and had a walk on the Downs. Then they had tea in the Fir Tree Café, a picturesque little place with oak beams and chintz curtains, colourful bowls of flowers on gate-legged tables, home-made scones and home-made cakes, and plenty of tea in the pot. It was very warm and cosy, they chatted and chuckled, and Stanley found he was enjoying it all enormously. Miss Williamson looked really beautiful with her dark soft hair and heart-shaped face. Ma-lee, they called her. He wondered how they spelt it.

After tea they went home again, to 16 Bridgefield Road, where her sisters and several other young people were gathered, playing table-tennis in the big billiard room. He enjoyed that too, especially when he and Miss Williamson played together. The day had turned out to be very different from what he had expected. Very different indeed. When the time came for him to leave Dr. Williamson offered to drive him to Norwood Junction station where he could get a train to New Cross, and Miss Williamson agreed to go with her father, for company. They said goodbye at the barrier, and as Stanley sat in the train it dawned on him that he was due to leave for the Congo in a fortnight's time, and he might never see her again.

The next day he was so restless that Winifred, who noticed the change in her usually imperturbable brother, asked him point blank what was the matter with him? What had happened at the home of the General Foreign Secretary of the Baptist Missionary Society? Had something gone wrong?

'It's that girl,' he admitted. 'I can't get her out of my mind.' He'd never known anything like this before. That vivid picture memory of his had always been under his control, the pictures recorded and stored away until they were summoned forth at his will. But now the pictures so clearly imprinted yesterday refused to be tucked away. He remembered what she looked like sitting in the car, with that big picture hat shading her face . . . walking over the Downs . . . smiling over the tea . . . flushed over the games . . . saying goodbye with a sudden quiet dignity, as though holding herself in check . . .

'Can't get her out of my mind,' he said. And there was no likelihood of meeting her again before he went back to the Congo.

Winifred looked at her brother, and realised he was in deadly earnest. She had never seen him like this about a girl before.

'Why don't you write to her?' she said. 'Tell her you'd like to see her again.' He'd get nowhere if he remained silent! 'Write to her!'

Stanley hesitated. 'I don't know how to spell her name,'

he admitted. 'Ma-lee it sounded like—but how do you spell that?'

'Well, just call her Mollie,' replied his practical sister. 'She'll understand.'

So Stanley went off to write the letter. It had all happened so suddenly and unexpectedly he scarcely admitted even to himself that he had fallen in love.

For Mali it was quite different. She too was writing a letter, a polite little note about the meeting he was booked to speak at in her church in a few days' time. She was sorry she would not be able to attend. The school in which she taught had been evacuated to Windsor due to the war, she explained, so she could only get home to Sutton at weekends. As missionary secretary she gave him a few necessary details about the meeting, and expressed the hope that it would be a good one.

It was all she could do. She couldn't tell him that she'd been interested in him ever since she heard him speak at that meeting in Bloomsbury before he went to the Congo. That she'd read the bits about him in the Baptist Missionary magazine with avidity, had gone to hear him speak two or three times since he returned, had met him briefly after church one Sunday when he was spending the weekend with Mrs. Moorshead (had he remembered that, she wondered) and that yesterday had been the most wonderful day in her life. Of course she could not tell him all that, or how she had felt as she said goodbye to him, seen him going out of her life again, back to Africa.

Of course she could not tell him all that. All she could do was to send him that polite little note, secretly hoping that he would reply, and then she could write to him when he was back in the Congo. As missionary secretary it would seem a reasonable thing to do, though she didn't even mention that, either.

The two letters crossed. After that everything went as smoothly as a well-oiled engine.

Mali wrote suggesting that he might be able to fit in a visit to Windsor to see her.

Stanley replied by return, fixing a date.

They met the following Saturday and spent most of the day walking and talking in Windsor Park. It was remarkable, how much they had in common. They found they were both free on the morning of April 3rd, a week before he was due to leave, and agreed to meet again then.

At ten-thirty a.m. on that day Dr. Williamson had a phone call from Windsor. Stanley Browne calling. He wanted to ask Dr. Williamson's permission to marry his daughter Mali, as she had just agreed to become his wife.

*   *   *

It had all happened in less than a fortnight, yet with such a precision and sense of fitness that neither had a moment's doubt but that it was appointed by God. The more they prayed and the more they talked together, the deeper was the assurance that they were intended for each other. For Mali it was the fulfilment of a hope she had scarcely dared to express even to herself, yet which had held her through the impressionable years of her early twenties when she might otherwise have been drawn to someone else. For Stanley, coming so soon after that memorable afternoon when he had renounced any right to married life if that was his Master's will, the joy of finding that 'the loveliest lady in the world' had been prepared for him was inexpressible. He set off on the journey back to Yakusu on 10th April 1940 with her photograph in his breast pocket and the prospect of preparing a home for her enlivening all he did.

The journey proved an eventful one, though it nearly ended in disaster. He escorted Winifred to Antwerp where she left by sea for missionary work in the Congo. His former landlady, eager and smiling, met him there and saw him off on the train into France. In Marseilles he boarded a fourteen-seater plane to Algiers where he came across a Salvation Army meeting in full swing, complete with band, bugles and drums. When the officer in charge of the meeting enquired if any of the onlookers wanted to testify to their faith, Stanley stepped forward. He was both willing and ready to do so.

'So once again in Africa I was able to testify in French to the Lord Jesus Christ and His saving power and keeping grace. Then we all sang together, "Thine be the glory, risen, conquering Son!" '

The next lap of the journey landed them in a little oasis in the middle of the Sahara, in time for lunch. Then back into the plane, en route for the Fort Lamy airport, near Lake Chad.

'And thereby hangs a story, for we couldn't find Fort Lamy. The visibility was reduced to less than one kilometre, and we had been flying at a height of fourteen thousand feet, without oxygen, when the pilot and radio operator came out to the passengers and said, "We advise you to fasten your safety belts. We can't get a reply from the radio station at Fort Lamy. No signal at all. If we can't spot the airport we shall have to make a forced landing in the scrub, and hope for the best." '

So there was Stanley, having so short a time before been contemplating the prospect of marrying Mali, preparing for a crash landing in the southern Sahara, not knowing whether it would be the end of him! His silent prayers for himself and his fellow-travellers were urgent and tinged with surprise—could it really be that he and Mali were not to be married after all? It seemed strangely incomplete, to be finishing his life now.

The tension lasted for over half an hour as the plane descended to three thousand feet and circled slowly round while the radio operator tried frantically to make contact with Fort Lamy.

'We've only got fuel enough for ten more minutes in the air,' the pilot announced grimly, peering through the haze. 'Fasten your belts!'

Then suddenly he gave an exclamation, and revved the

engines. The passengers stiffened with surprise. What was that he had said?

'There's Lake Chad! They've spotted it! And the airport . . . He's going to land there, after all . . .' The plane cruised down, taxied along the tarmac, and came safely to a standstill.

At that point it became evident why no message had been received from the Fort Lamy radio operator—he was dead drunk, reeling towards the plane with a stupid grin on his face.

He looked even more stupid when the Captain, keyed up with the strain of that perilous flight, shouted angrily and landed him a violent crack on the chin before the District Commissioner, who was also there, could stop him . . .

Stanley spent that night in the home of a missionary of the Christian Brethren. He had been in Fort Lamy for years, translating portions of the Bible into the languages of some of the near-by oases, and said rather sadly, 'The people here are very unresponsive. I don't know of a single person I've led to Christ all the time I've been here.' Stanley's mind flew to Yakusu with its crowded church, to the little Christian meeting-places in the villages, to the fresh-faced young *infirmiers* preparing to serve Christ among their own people. The contrast between that fruitful area and this arid desert land was very marked in every way, and the evening he spent with that lonely, steadfast Brethren missionary was imprinted in his memory.*

The rest of the journey was uneventful. Raymond Holmes was at Stanleyville to meet him and convey him down-river to Yakusu. The drums rumbled and the villagers came out to shout a welcome as the motor-boat shot by, and Stanley

---

* Years later Dr. Browne was in Kano, North Nigeria, and met a number of people who had come from the Fort Lamy area in search of work, and settled there. Several of them were attached to the local Gospel Hall, '. . . fine young Christians who were the result of the faithful sowing of the Word of God into their own language by that lone, lonely and disappointed missionary.'

waved back, pleased to be among them again. There was much to talk about, although Stanley remained silent about his engagement. He sprung that news on everyone later on, when all the missionary team was gathered together for an informal chat on one of the verandahs. On the boat, speeding downstream, the conversation was mainly about the progress of the work, the buying of this new motor-boat, and the triumphant opening of the new maternity ward in the hospital.

'Pity you weren't here for it,' said Holmes. 'A military band, a special steamer for the Governor and all sorts of important people from Stanleyville. It was a tremendous reception.

'Had a bit of trouble, of course—mainly from the local midwives, who saw themselves being put out of business. Hope we can bring down the mortality rate among babies now.

'Notice that clearing there?' he said suddenly. Stanley's eyes followed his outstretched arm, pointing to the opposite bank of the river.

'Yalisombo. The camp for people with leprosy—the first colony in the district. We've made a start at last, clearing the ground. It isn't going to be easy to persuade them to leave their villages and their families and come and live there. Even though we provide them with shelter, and help them with tools and things for cultivating the land, and of course they know they'll get the best medical treatment we can give them when they're ill.

'All the same,' he said with a sigh. 'I don't know really how satisfied they will be with the arrangement. It's the only way we can get the disease under control, segregating them like this, but you can't expect them to see it that way. They'd rather be back in their own villages, even though they know they're better off here.

'And of course they know we haven't got a cure . . .'

'We know it, too,' said Stanley wryly. 'No cure for leprosy—not yet.'

He didn't know anything about the chemical compound that had been synthesised from a formula produced by a couple of German chemists a few months after he was born. It had come to light and was being studied in a hospital in Louisiana, U.S.A.

In the early Church the divine interest in and concern for bodily as well as spiritual health were generally recognised. We have the well-known instruction in James concerning the anointing of the sick person with oil: 'and the prayer of faith shall save the sick.' In course of time, however, the connection between 'wholeness' and 'holiness' became lost, and the superstitions and wonder-seeking of the degenerate Church were the results of its rigid attachment to an unscientific system. When science in general and medicine in particular were liberated from these ecclesiastical chains, the original happy relationships between bodily and spiritual health were virtually forgotten.

Then, the wheel of history coming full-circle again, we note that the first missionary to leave these shores as the result of the missionary re-awakening in eighteenth-century Protestantism was a medical man, John Thomas, who sailed for India as a missionary of the B.M.S. in 1793. When William Carey was asked if he was willing to go to India with Thomas, 'he readily answered in the affirmative'. Thomas's own contribution to the beginnings of modern missions has been dwarfed, of course, by Carey's prodigious work in so many spheres, but we remember with gratitude that it was Dr. Thomas' medical skill in reducing a dislocated shoulder that played an important part in the conversion of the patient, Krishna Pal, who was the first fruits of the mission.

In China it was a medical missionary, Peter Parker, who was one of the pioneers who introduced that vast country to the benefits of medicine and the blessings of the Gospel . . . In Africa, of course, the outstanding name is that of Dr. David Livingstone . . .

Medical missions today form an integral part of the Christian missionary enterprise, at once an expression of the infinite compassion of God for His suffering creatures, and an aspect of the message that Jesus came to bring.

S.G.B.
1946
(*Extract from* The Baptist Times)

CHAPTER SEVEN

Into the forest

Big Ben was striking, one . . . two . . . three . . ., deliberate and unhurried, and little groups of people all over the world leaned over their radio sets to listen to the nine o'clock news. Britain was blacked out. Not a chink of light escaped through the heavily curtained windows, the streets were in darkness, air-raid warnings shrieked, planes roared overhead, and Big Ben chimed on.

Four . . . five . . . six. The deep tones echoed solemnly in comfortable, well-furnished rooms in the free world, while in attics and basements in Nazi-occupied Europe men with their fingers on the controls laid their ears close to the little receiving sets, fearful that the sounds would be heard outside.

Seven . . . eight . . . nine . . .

Under a star-filled African sky, on the banks of the Congo, Stanley walked briskly up the steps of 'bachelors' house' to join the group that had gathered in Kenneth Parkinson's bedroom to listen to the news over the only radio in Yakusu. It had become a nightly rendezvous for all the missionaries on the station, this one link with the storm centre in which most of those they loved the dearest were battling for survival. 'This is London . . .' and then the news, given with the stark, unemotional calmness that seems to characterise the English when their backs are against the wall.

And their backs were against the wall all right, that summer of 1940! Holland, Belgium and Luxembourg had been invaded in May, and so swift had been the Nazi advance that by the end of the month the entire British

Expeditionary Force of nearly half a million men had retreated for what was to become known as the epic of Dunkirk. By the middle of June Paris had been occupied, the French had capitulated and Winston Churchill had broadcast that Great Britain and the British Empire stood alone. By the end of July the Battle of Britain had started. Flotillas of enemy ships were preparing for the invasion of the island, and throughout August there were almost daily reports of battles on the seas, battles in the air, with raids on military targets, then raids over London.

Day and night, raids over London . . .

They listened silently in the tropical night, the little group of missionaries in Yakusu, their faces grave. Letters from home continued to come spasmodically, often weeks old, though many were lost, and even those that got through only contained incomplete news. Security was tight. Word had been received that a party of five, Mr. and Mrs. Parris, Mr. and Mrs. Ennals, and Miss Mali Williamson were expected to leave England for the Belgian Congo early in September, but no information about the date of departure or means of transport could be given, so when, on the thirteenth of the month the headline news was the fierce bombing of London, even of Buckingham Palace itself, Stanley did not know whether Mali was still in England or not.

It was well for his peace of mind that he had not seen her that day. She had suddenly been instructed to be at Paddington station at eight a.m. the next morning, with all her luggage, ready to depart, and there remained one vitally important matter she had been unable to complete. She still had to get the censor to pass and seal the documents required so that she could be legally married to Stanley Browne according to Belgian law in the Congo.

There was no time for delay. Air raid or no air raid, she was determined to get those documents if it were humanly possible to do so. With prayer in her heart, and the necessary papers firmly clutched in her handbag, she set off for the

West End. She was at Clapham Junction when the first air-raid siren sounded. From then on she struggled in and out of Underground stations, along rubble-strewn streets, taking cover as planes roared overhead, the crashing of masonry deafening her, wondering if the censor's office would still be standing by the time she got there . . . When she eventually reached home that night she had in her possession the necessary papers, all duly passed by the censor, but they were valid only until 15 November, 1940. If she wasn't married to Stanley by that time, the process would have to start all over again.

As for Stanley, the routine of life in Yakusu had been speeded up. On top of the work in the hospital, the training of the *infirmiers*, the correspondence course, the preaching, the periodical journeys to the forest, he had to make arrangements for the vaccination against smallpox of thousands of people in his district. This most dreaded of all diseases in the Congo had flared up in the district and been traced to Stanleyville, where a man had died of it. Unknown to the hospital authorities until it was too late, his corpse was stolen by his relatives, who wanted to bury it in his home village. The man's body was taken down-river by canoe, duly given a ceremonial funeral, and buried. Within a fortnight smallpox had broken out in the area, unwittingly spread by people who travelled to other villages, and there was the threat of a widespread epidemic in which thousands might die, or be permanently blinded.

Obtaining the vaccine from Kisenyi in Eastern Congo, and storing it in refrigerators and thermos flasks was only the beginning of the campaign to arrest the disease. People had to be notified to come to a certain place at a certain time for medical attention, then they had to be persuaded to allow the doctors to scratch their arms with needles (a highly suspicious procedure, what would it lead to?), and finally prevented from rubbing lime juice on the scratches or exposing them to the sunlight. And when the sores appeared, it was not easy to convince everyone that that was just as it should be, and that the scabs should not be rubbed away or treated with local medicine. By the time some hundred thousand people had been vaccinated the medical team at Yakusu was exhausted—but an epidemic had been averted. Stanley had vaccinated himself dozens of times to show the people he was not afraid of the medicine.

For him there had been the added activity of preparing a home for Mali, anxiety about her safety, and apprehension about the outcome of the war. Although far from the actual scenes of the conflict, the work in Yakusu and the other mission centres was inevitably being affected. The British authorities had warned them that it might be necessary to evacuate their stations and travel to the east coast, though by what means they were to get there was not specified. 'The Red Devil, I suppose!' said Holmes with a wry grin, looking at the Chevrolet they had been able to buy at a reduced price because of its colour. 'Though how we're going to get everybody in it, then travel thousands of miles over dirt roads, and no petrol stations, I don't know!' They decided that the time to worry about making that journey would be when it had to be made, and not before, but there were some things that demanded immediate action. The blockade on freight and passenger ships, most of which travelled in convoy guarded by the Royal Navy, was resulting in a diminished and uncertain supply of stores and medicines, and things were likely to get worse.

'We'll have to be our own producers,' Stanley decided, and made a prompt start on the garden of the bungalow that was being allotted to him. Beds were dug in the vegetable garden, covered with palm-fronds to protect the soil from the torrents of rain that poured down in sudden tropical storms, and before long a healthy growth was evident under the energetic hands of African schoolboys eager to earn a little money. He had managed to buy seeds of tomato, lettuce, carrot, leek and other vegetables not seen before in that part of the Congo, and was confident that Mali would soon have an adequate supply for her housekeeping needs when she arrived. Later on there would be fruit as well, for he had planted seeds and cuttings of fruit trees in what came to be known as 'The Browne Orchard'.

. . . If she arrived. There was always the haunting fear that she would be one of the victims of those merciless air raids, or that the ship on which she travelled would be sunk by German submarines. Winifred had come through safely enough, but she had got away earlier.

There were, however, too many other things to be thought of to give much time for brooding. Medicines had to be obtained somehow, and that involved exploring new sources of supply.

'We're going to need a lot of the chaulmoogra oil for the leprosy patients,' he said to Holmes as they were talking together about the leprosarium which they hoped to open soon at Yalisombo. They were eager to get on with it now that the smallpox epidemic had subsided. It was a new venture but of primary importance in view of the prevalence of the disease.

'A lot of chaulmoogra oil,' said Holmes slowly. Then he lapsed into silence, and Stanley, sensing that something was coming waited expectantly. Holmes looked as though he had an idea, and if he had, then Stanley must be the one to carry it out. He had learned that it usually happened that way. Holmes was the man of vision, he was the man of action. It was a good working partnership.

'I wonder if we could produce our own oil,' said Holmes. 'They grow chaulmoogra trees in India. Why not here?'

So that was it. 'A plantation of chaulmoogra trees!' said Stanley briskly. 'We'll see what we can do. Find a site—get the men onto clearing it—import some seeds . . .' his mind moved quickly, seeing the possibilities, and what needed to be done. It would mean a lot of extra correspondence, and studying of instructions, obtaining land and overseeing workmen, but he was prepared for that. Eventually they would have their own supply of the oil that had proved effective in treating some of the milder forms of leprosy.

They would need it. Plans were going ahead for the official opening of the leprosarium in Yalisombo with the co-operation of the Belgian authorities in running it. Holmes and Stanley had visited Stanleyville several times to see the senior administrator about it, and he had given his full approval to the project, promising that a supply of food should be provided for the inmates. It would help to augment what they could produce by their own efforts. The medical side of things would be the responsibility of the doctors.

Meanwhile the war raged on, communications with England were infrequent and uncertain, and nothing had been heard of Mali for weeks. For Stanley, the worst times in that period were when he had to go on his trips into the forest, cycling hour after hour in the green half-light, so conscious of his loneliness and anxiety that he wanted to scream. It was easier at Yakusu with people around all the time, making constant demands on his attention, but those long lonely journeys left him a prey to gloomy forebodings. If Mali were killed! If the years ahead had to be spent like this, without her, without the prospect of seeing her, hearing from her, he wondered how he could endure them.

Why art thou cast down, o my soul? And why art thou disquieted within me? Hope thou in God . . .

It is a good thing to talk to oneself on occasion. The Psalmist had done so, taking himself to task for his lack of faith. Thousands of years later, in the depths of the Topoke forest, Stanley did likewise. *Hope thou in God.* The inward fight against depression was a fierce one in those days, and was not won in a single battle, but it came to an end during the last week of October, when word was received that a party of five, including Miss Mali Williamson, had arrived in the Belgian Congo. They had been over six weeks at sea, their liner having been diverted almost as far west as New York, then south towards Cape Town, before eventually mooring at Boma, a port on the north bank of the Congo, a few miles from the equator. A train journey, then a thousand miles up the Congo had yet to be traversed, and there was only a monthly river-steamer service, but the day came when four loud blasts from the river announced the arrival of passengers. Stanley, running down to the little quay, had eyes for only one of them. There was Mali at last, in a flowered frock and a shady maroon hat, smiling at him across the water.

'*Kalibo, ino batotina!*' she said to the Africans who flocked round to greet her, and a loud murmur of admiration went up as they exclaimed,

'Why, she can speak Lokele already!'

'I had plenty of time on the boat for lessons,' she explained later. 'And Mrs. Ennals was the best possible teacher to give them. She was quite a martinet when it came to homework.' Stanley did not say much, but the satisfaction in his heart deepened. He had, after all, met her only half-a-dozen times before, and had had little opportunity to discover her ability in practical matters, or to observe how she spent her spare time. So she had got right down to studying the local language, and she was not afraid to use it. It was evident that she intended to be a missionary in her own right, that she would not expect merely to settle in as a housewife, and he glowed at the prospect of having such a life partner. Her presence with him would transform the tedium of those journeys in the forest, and at last there would be someone who could mix with the women there, talk to them, enter into their lives and help them in a way he never could.

The arrival of Mali on 13 November had only one drawback, but it threatened to be an embarrassing one. The papers whereby she and Stanley could be legally married in Belgian territory, which she had braved the blitz in London to obtain two months previously, would be invalid after the 15th. Twenty-four hours' notice must be given in Stanley-ville, and as it was already too late to do it the day she arrived at Yakusu, it would have to be done on the morrow. This left only one day, the 14th. And the 15th was a public holiday. All the government offices would be closed, and there would be no one to perform the ceremony.

Before daybreak on the 14th Stanley boarded the Mission launch and arrived in Stanleyville as the offices were opening. He was a well-known figure there, and had no difficulty in obtaining an audience with the senior administrator. He explained his problem.

'Dr. Browne,' said the friendly official immediately. 'You have done so much for us, I am glad of the opportunity to do something for you. This office shall be opened tomorrow, and I myself will marry you to your Mademoiselle.' He was even better than his word, arriving for the short ceremony in full regalia, sash and ribbons and all. Mali duly made all the responses necessary under the Belgian law, promising to follow her husband wherever he went and make her home with him, casting a merry glance with just the slightest suspicion of a wink of the left eye at Stanley as she did so. He grinned back. It was a light-hearted affair, soon over, and they hurried back to Yakusu for the wedding in the church, when they would plight their troth in the sight of God and man. The place was packed, of course, and a sea of black faces turned to look at a perfect English bride veiled in white walk slowly up the aisle to stand beside their young *Bonganga*. Fellow-missionaries had united their talents to make this, the first European wedding in Yakusu, as beautiful as possible and one of them, who was a wizard at the organ, delighted everyone as he produced a wedding march that throbbed with the familiar music of the drums.

Even the large wedding cake which Mali had brought with her from England looked all right. The ants had got at it, but knowledgeable missionary housewives had gently re-baked it to encourage them to flee the city of their destruction, and Winifred had spent a couple of hours carefully extracting corpses before going to don her bridesmaid's dress.

The honeymoon was spent at Yalemba, one hundred miles by motor-boat down-river, at the last of the string of B.M.S. mission stations founded by the famous George Grenfell. Stanley was a regular visitor there for the control of sleeping sickness, and his arrival with his bride was the occasion for a good deal of unaccustomed social life and sightseeing. A honeymoon cottage had been prepared with an archway of palm fronds leading up to it from the bank of the river. Belgian and English friends who looked upon Stanley as their family doctor were lavish with invitations to dinners and parties, while on the mission station itself every household wanted to entertain the newly-married couple.

Stanley's versatile gifts ranging from medicine to music, and being first and foremost a missionary, 'I could not entirely deprive myself of the right to work while on a honeymoon,' he wrote later. 'And of course the good friends at Yalemba had lined up the sleeping sickness patients and others on whom they wanted a medical opinion. So on the first day of our honeymoon there we were bang straight into the work again, looking at cerebro-spinal fluid and hunting for trypanosomes, prescribing treatment and doing a few minor operations.' Typically he entered into the purposeful life of the community, more at home speaking at meetings and helping to train the choir than engaging in superficial conversation at social gatherings, which he attended politely, immaculately dressed, but unobtrusively withdrawing from the centre of animated chatter and listening as others talked. On more than one occasion the guest of honour could be seen as a friendly onlooker, very fluent in French, but accustomed to thinking on more serious topics.

Mali seemed to fit in everywhere. He marvelled as he watched her, heard her speaking as readily in French as in English, equally at ease among the sophisticated Belgian planters and the workers on their plantations. She listened more than she talked, giving her full attention to the one she was with, nodding sympathetically now and then, never ruffled or bored. She was wonderful! Everybody liked her, that was evident, and he glowed with pride as now and then he caught her eye in an intimate, understanding glance while she continued her conversation uninterrupted.

She, on her part, secretly observing him, noticed that

without any evident embarrassment he declined alcohol with a smile and a quiet 'Thank you, I don't drink,' and closed his eyes at the commencement of a meal, silently giving thanks to God for it, whatever company he was in. She was glad he did that. It was the way her father acted, too. Without even having to discuss it each realised that the simple piety which had permeated their parents' lives would be continued in their own. The hymn he had chosen to translate into Lokele for their wedding had struck just the right note.

'O happy home, where Thou art loved the dearest . . .'

On a more practical level she found with relief that he knew what to do when a snake slithered suddenly and silently across the floor, and how to deal with the insects that found their way under the mosquito net at night. 'All but the midges,' he said ruefully scratching his neck. 'They're so small they get through the mesh, and there's nothing to be done about it but endure it!'

He had a way of making history come alive, too. 'That hand was one which grasped a spear when fifty-six war canoes set out to attack H.M. Stanley in 1877,' he told her after she had shaken hands with a very old African at a church service one Sunday. 'They weren't only going to kill him,' he added with his quizzical grin. 'They were going to eat him, too!'

Sightseeing included a visit to the *Huileries du Conge Belge* at Elisabetha and evoked a rather solemn reaction. On the huge plantations of oil-palm trees they watched sweating workmen climbing nimbly up the trees to cut the bunches of palm-nuts for processing in the factories that had been built on the site, saw the oil being extracted and poured into drums ready for transportation to Europe, noted the labour involved.

'All this to provide us Westerners with soap and margarine!' said Stanley reflectively as he watched the perspiring black figures working in the heat of the day. 'How much we depend on them for our food and our comfort! We owe them a lot. It's our duty, no more, to do something for them in return. I'm glad we can help them medically as well as spiritually.'

The carefree days came to an end rather abruptly when, shortly after going to bed one night, they were awakened by a loud cough that announced the arrival of an unexpected visitor.

'What is it?' called Stanley.

'A message from Yakusu—something urgent.'

Stanley switched on his torch, glanced carefully around to ensure there were no snakes or scorpions anywhere, crawled out from under the mosquito net and went to the window. 'A paddler has just brought these from Dr. Holmes,' he was told and handed a bundle of letters. On top was one addressed to him in Holmes's familiar handwriting. He tore it open, read it through quickly, then turned to Mali.

'We'll have to go back to Yakusu as soon as possible,' he said. 'Yellow fever—a plantation manager has just died of it. If an epidemic breaks out it will be ghastly. We've got to stop it spreading. Holmes has been in touch with the government medical officers and there's vaccine on the way, but it'll be a full-time job getting everybody vaccinated.

'He's been in touch with the Rockefeller Foundation, too. They're going to send some of their experts to make investigations.'

The next day they returned to Yakusu. The vaccine arrived and so did the scientists from the Rockefeller Foundation. Then the widespread Yakusu medical team sprang into action, with daily temperatures taken and recorded in scores of scattered villages. Nothing of a very dramatic nature seemed to emerge from it all. The threatened Yellow Fever epidemic was averted. As for the investigations, it was eventually discovered that there had been several waves of Yellow Fever in the district during the previous twenty years, but no one had realised it because it was a sub-clinical form that didn't kill people. What new medical knowledge the Rockefeller Foundation actually obtained from the laboratories they set up and the serum they collected and the mice they injected was reported in the medical press. The knowledge they obtained in one realm, however, was to have a significant bearing on Stanley's later career. The thing that impressed them was that in a remote region of one of the most backward countries in Africa, local boys had been so efficiently trained that they were able to take methodically and record accurately some 10,000 temperatures of Africans scattered in rural areas every morning for weeks. It was, perhaps, the most surprising discovery the Rockefeller Foundation experts made while doing research into Yellow Fever in the Congo.

Once back in Yakusu the Brownes soon settled into a routine so full that they rarely saw each other except at mealtimes. Mali's teaching training and experience found an outlet both in the girls' school and in helping the medical auxiliaries with arithmetic, French and hygiene, while Stanley as always had his days and his evenings occupied in the hospital and at his desk. He played a hard-hitting game of tennis on Saturday afternoons, to let off steam, but as soon as it was over he was back again on the job. Only when his turn came round to go off to the Topeke forest to visit the *infirmiers* were he and Mali together every day and all day, for Mali went with him, manfully carrying her bicycle over streams and fallen trees when she wasn't riding it after him along the slippery paths. When they arrived at their destination she was soon surrounded by women, eager to see this strange white-skinned member of their own sex, who spoke to them about God and Jesus, could read books and teach them to sing hymns. *Bonganga*'s wife was like a visitant from another planet, yet in a remarkable way proved to be very like themselves, to understand them, and to have a sometimes quite disconcerting knowledge of their innermost thoughts and feelings. She had come into a very fruitful field of service made ready to her hand, and although the physical discomforts were sometimes intense, and frequently irksome, those periodic journeys in the forest were happy and carefree for her as well as for Stanley. So it was with a mixture of joy and apprehension that, as they were preparing for another trip which would take them away for several weeks, it dawned on her that everything wasn't normal with her physically, and that she ought to tell Stanley about it.

'Stanley,' she said, 'I think I may be going to have a baby.'

Joy at the prospect was somewhat clouded by the thought of that journey through the forest—the hours of strenuous cycling, the heaving of bicycles over obstacles of all kinds, the exposure to violent tropical storms that would drench to the skin within a minute. They looked at each other questioningly. Ought she to make this journey? Would it be putting the unborn child at risk? They discussed it for a while, then quite simply acted as they always did when uncertain about anything.

'Let's pray about it, and ask the Lord what He wants us to do.' With bowed heads they laid the case before Him, then went on with their different tasks as before, waiting for the direction they expected from Him. Maybe some circumstances would occur which would hinder Mali's going, perhaps some advice would come from an unexpected quarter, or something in their daily Bible reading would reveal the right course to take. When they came together again to make their decision they found they had nothing special to go on except the thought of all those people in the forests and plantations who were expecting them, needy people wanting the help they could give.

Whoso saveth his life shall lose it; and whoso loseth his life for My sake and the gospel's, the same shall find it. This was the principle which had dominated their lives for years, and they were not surprised to find it was still their guiding star.

'I'll go, and trust the Lord to keep me safe,' said Mali. They were away for seven weeks, and the travelling was as difficult as ever, but she returned none the worse for it, and very certain now that she was to be a mother.

The main purpose of that particular trip, apart from the routine medical work, had been to discover the people suffering from leprosy and persuade the infectious cases to move into the leprosarium at Yalisombo. Very few were prepared to do so. They preferred to stay at home among their own people, who were willing enough to have them provided they could still work. There was no social stigma connected with the disease in the minds of the Congolese, and the only reason why leprous people were turned out or abandoned was because they were no longer able to fulfil their normal functions.

'What use is she to me now? She can't have more children, she can't work,' was not considered an unnatural attitude for a husband to adopt towards his wife. 'She is useless. Let her go. I'll get another wife.' Or in the case of a man, 'He can't do anything with his hands any more and his legs are stumps. He can't even walk properly. Why should he eat the food other people have worked for and hunted for? Send him away!' If they were able to work they could stay, living alongside their families and spreading their disease unnoticed. The very slowness of leprosy to show itself, then the apparent unimportance of those patches on the skin, prevented anyone from taking it seriously. It wasn't a killer like smallpox or sleeping sickness or malaria. So why move away to this place far away on the river where the white men wanted to segregate them?

It took a great deal of explanation and persuasion on the part of Holmes as well as Stanley to convince anyone that the move ought to be made. Warnings about the perils of infection, especially to children, had little effect. The prospect of leprosy being eventually stamped out in the next generation elicited no enthusiasm in the present one. The leprosarium at Yalisombo was getting off to a very slow start. The site had been cleared, neat little wattle-and-daub huts had been built for the patients, each with its own patch of garden, a communal plantation would provide rice and maize, an *infirmier* and his wife would be on the spot to help at all times, and the *Benganga* from Yakusu would cross the river once a week to give medical attention to anyone requiring it. These inducements proved sufficiently attractive for a few to come and try it out, though some insisted on bringing their families as well, posing a new problem. Somehow a way must be found to segregate the healthy from the diseased within the leprosarium itself. What was to be done?

Before a solution had been found, however, the whole thing had come to an end. Less than three months after the official opening the place was empty. The inmates had all drifted away, the last batch having departed the night before the doctor's weekly visit from Yakusu. When Stanley's canoe grounded on the beach that morning, the only people left in the leprosarium were the bewildered and crestfallen *infirmier* and his wife.

'Gone! All gone!' they wailed. 'We tried to stop them but we couldn't. They'd got it all planned and went last night. They said there wasn't enough food, and your medicine was no good, and they weren't going to stay any longer, so they went. All gone!'

A thing that we cannot do without is fresh air. People can do without food for about three weeks, without water for three days, without air for three minutes. Because we breathe without thinking about it we forget that the taking of fresh air into our lungs is of the first importance.

When we come to the 'health of the heart' Christians often forget this. They think about food for the heart, and about exercise in Christian service, but they forget that they must constantly breathe the fresh air of the Spirit if they are to have spiritual health . . . The Christian has to breathe good fresh air in the spiritual sense if he is to keep healthy. He must be able to get into his spiritual lungs something that will carry strength and health to every part of his being. Prayer is this 'something'. It is a kind of spiritual air, which we must breathe if we are to keep alive. It is the contact of our spirits with God.

S.G.B.
1949.
(*From the booklet* The Hygiene of the Heart
*published by The Sheldon Press, Northumberland
Avenue, London W.C.2*).

CHAPTER EIGHT

A Price to be paid

You couldn't travel in the Belgian Congo in the early 1940s without being aware of the flies. And the fleas. And the mosquitoes. And the perspiration. And the drums. John Latouche was conscious of them all as he travelled down-river from Stanleyville early in 1943, wondering what awaited him in Yakusu where he was to be shown round by some Protestant missionaries reputedly of the Bible-thumping type. Not at all the sort of people he was accustomed to! He supposed they would be gaunt and severe-looking, dressed in black, like the caricatures of them produced in sophisticated magazines, and inwardly braced himself for the encounter. It wouldn't be for long, he was only going for the day, and after all everything is grist for the writer's mill. He'd been told that the Baptist medical mission in Yakusu was a model of its kind, playing an important role in the health programme of the country, so he had decided to pay it a visit.

The drums reported his progress down-river, for foreign visitors from afar were rare in those years, and when he arrived at the jetty a sort of African reception committee was ready for him, eager to escort him up the steps to the short promenade with the bungalows where *Bonganga* and Mama Browne lived. It was there he got his first surprise. The young couple who greeted him were smiling, not severe, their faces fresh, not gaunt, and they were dressed, not in black but in shorts and open-necked shirt and floral dress, looking a good deal cooler and cleaner than he felt himself to be. They led him into their simple dining-room with

131

unselfconscious ease, talking as naturally as if they were entertaining him in a London suburb. The table was tastefully laid, a smiling, immaculately clad young African waited on them, and the food was excellent.

Mali did not mention that she had delved recklessly into her most carefully guarded food store to provide that meal, and that fellow-missionaries had come to the rescue with some of the ingredients she didn't have. No need to draw attention to the difficulties missionaries encountered in getting suitable provisions especially during the war. She couldn't disguise the fact that his was the very first name in their visitor's book, though. It was presented to him to sign in all its pristine glory—two pieces of brown cardboard bound together with red sticking tape, enclosing leaves of white paper carefully put together in the Yakusu printing press when it was known that a famous American writer was coming. And by the time he'd eaten their food and drunk their tea and chatted and laughed, observing with inward surprise how happy they were, John Latouche was quite in the mood to sign their book with a flourish.

'To Dr. and Mrs. Browne,' he wrote. 'Gratitude for a good meal and good fellowship.' And after his name he drew a merry little sketch of a fat flying angel to embellish it. *Semper aliquid novum ex Africa*,' he added. 'Always something new out of Africa.'

They took him over to the hospital and what he noticed was not only the appearance of the patients, who to his unaccustomed eyes seemed pathetically thin and ravaged with disease, but the compassionate way Stanley and Mali looked at them. They really cared about these people! This charming, cultured couple who could so obviously have chosen a pleasanter way of life, voluntarily spending their years in this remote area, this tiny outpost of civilisation— what made them do it? He met the other members of the missionary community, saw the orderly classes of bright-faced African children, heard them singing in a language he didn't know the familiar spiritual 'Swing low, sweet chariot' and admitted after it was all over that it had been like visiting another planet. He couldn't account for it. There was such a purposefulness, such a cheerfulness, such simplicity and sincerity about them all. The background from which he had come, New York with its sophistication and cynicism, hadn't prepared him for this sort of thing. He made no claim to being a religious man, he said, but he had seen at Yakusu the Christian spirit in action, and it had made an indelible impression.

He was even more surprised when someone said to him later, 'That surgeon, Browne. He's very well qualified, you know. He's got F.R.C.S. and M.R.C.P., and a whole string of other letters after his name.' With all that knowledge and training and the opportunities that must have been open to him, to be burying himself in that vast green backwater in the Congo—and apparently enjoying it! It was past his comprehension, the American writer confessed, but he couldn't help admiring it.

For Stanley and Mali his visit provided a touch with the outside world that was enlivening, for they had not been away from Yakusu and its district since they were married. An occasional brief visit to Stanleyville was the nearest they got to Western civilisation. Not that they missed it. When Latouche had asked Mali if she missed London she had answered indifferently, 'No, not much. Of course, it would be nice to go back for a holiday after the war, if we ever get time.' Then she had added with a little sigh, 'There's so little time out here!'

The days were full, but they were satisfying in spite of continuing anxiety about the progress of the war and the increasing difficulty in obtaining supplies. The arrival of their first child three weeks ahead of schedule had been heralded with enthusiasm and excitement throughout the district, adding to the general flurry and fervour occasioned by the hundred and fiftieth anniversary celebrations of the Baptist Missionary Society. The drums rippled the news from village to village in ever-widening circles that *Bonganga*

Browne had a son. At the hospital prayer meeting the day he
was born one of the students prayed that God would protect
the little baby 'who can't tell up-river from down-river yet'.
When the little fellow was only a few months old they started
taking him into the district on their visits to the dispensaries,
for some roads had been built by this time, and it was
possible to travel to the nearer places in the Red Devil. The
appearance of a white baby drew the crowds and Mali had to
stand back, smiling bravely, while her child was handed
over to the old village chiefs who wanted to see him. One of
them, known to harbour nostalgic memories of the days
before the Belgian Government came and decreed there was
to be no more killing and eating of human flesh, looked
down gloatingly on what must have appeared to him a
particularly tender and tasty meal. 'What a nice, chubby
little boy!' he murmured, rubbing his hands together. Mali
was more than usually glad when she could get away politely,
Derek firmly clasped in her arms.

The whole of the vast district over which Holmes and
Stanley had the medical oversight was being opened up,
with the establishment of little schools as well as dispensaries. The young men who staffed the dispensaries had all
been trained at Yakusu and appointed to their positions not
only on account of their medical qualifications, but because
of their personal faith in Jesus Christ. They became the
spearhead of good medicine and evangelism in the areas
where they lived, and provided Stanley with unlimited
opportunities for preaching and teaching during his itinerations.

'It was a wonderful team effort. I journeyed with a team
of students from the hospital in Yakusu, and with the
medical auxiliary in charge of the local dispensary. In this
way we examined every person in every village every year.
At the same time we were able to meet with the people, live
with them, feed with them.

'They had a proverb that until you had been there for ten
years you were like a snake! Not a snake in the grass, but

one without an evident home in the district. You came, you glided through, you went away. But after you had been there ten years and spoke the local language, and could joke and laugh with the people, sitting round the camp fire in the evenings, then you were really accepted by them. You could gossip the Gospel and they would listen.' When Mali and little Derek accompanied him the drums were beaten more excitedly than ever, and the women came flocking to see her. There was one never-to-be-forgotten occasion when a hundred of them turned up to report that they had all been out on evangelistic trips to neighbouring villages, inspired to do so by a talk she had given them on letting their light shine.

There were encouragements in other ways, too. The Baptist Hospital in Yakusu was getting a name for itself by producing some of the best young medical auxiliaries in the Belgian Congo. Great was the rejoicing one year when all twelve of the students who set off for Stanleyville to take their final, the oral test, passed. In their clean white suits and with well-brushed hair they appeared before the government doctor, answering his questions without hesitation and with commendable self-control, although on the river journey back their feelings got the better of them and they shouted and waved flags with delirious excitement, announcing their success. On arrival at Yakusu, however, they regained control of themselves and with heads held high stood to attention like naval ratings as they sang 'Now thank we all our God, with hearts and hands and voices!' Stanley was proud of them. Inevitably there were some who started the course and for one reason or another failed to complete it, but there was no doubt about it, Yakusu's record was an exceptionally good one.

Everything was going well, it seemed, except the fight against leprosy. Sleeping sickness had practically disappeared, the last case being discharged cured in 1947, threatened epidemics of smallpox and yellow fever had been averted by prompt action and there were effective injections available for yaws. Even tuberculosis was on the decrease. But when it came to leprosy the position remained virtually unchanged. The notes Stanley kept so meticulously told of some patients whose leprosy had healed itself, not by medicine but simply because they were naturally resistant, their infection was a mere transient skin patch that eventually healed itself. Indeterminate leprosy. But there were some who had more chronic, well-defined patches that showed up clearly on dark skins—tuberculoid leprosy that could damage and eventually destroy nerves and lead to terrible ulcers and deformities. He kept a record of them all. The patches of numbness, the lumps, the ulcers, the deformities; the people in whom the disease was developing steadily, those in whom it was developing slowly, those in whom it seemed to be at a standstill. He took tiny scrapings of skin tissue, and nasal smears, and examined them under the microscope for those infinitesimal, rod-like germs that the Norwegian doctor, Hansen, had discovered in 1873, which had been medically classified as *Mycobacterium leprae* afterwards. He observed and he recorded, and he enthused the young medical auxiliaries to do the same, teaching them how to take smears, encouraging them to peer through the microscope and differentiate between the bacilli that were *Mycobacterium leprae* and those that were not. He taught them how to give the injections of chaulmoogra oil between the layers of the skin, a procedure from which everybody shrank because it was so excruciatingly painful. Stanley had to admit that it wasn't always very effective, either. It was the best they could do, however, and quite often it proved useful, providing it was administered regularly.

That was one of the main reasons for wanting patients to come into the leprosarium at Yalisombo—to ensure that they got regular treatment, and that they were cared for when they became incapacitated. It was not only for the purposes of segregation that the place had been opened and then re-opened.

For by this time another start had been made. He and

A PRICE TO BE PAID

Holmes, after the initial shock of disappointment at finding
the leprosarium completely deserted of patients that morning
in 1942, had decided not to accept defeat. Leprosy could not
be allowed to flourish unchallenged in the Congo. They
talked it over with Philip Austin, who had joined the medical
team at Yakusu, and faced the situation squarely. It would
be a long, long battle to stamp the disease out. Even if a
thousand of the contagious cases could be persuaded to come
and live in segregation in Yalisombo, it would take at least
twenty years for the disease to be brought under control. As
it was, the few score who had taken the plunge and come
hadn't been happy, hadn't been satisfied and eventually
they'd all gone back to their families and their villages, to
continue scattering those malevolent little bacilli every time
they sneezed.

'They didn't get all the food they wanted—that was the
chief complaint,' the *infirmier* in charge had reported. 'If
only there had been more food they might have stayed. They
said they didn't eat as well as when they were in their own
villages, and that if they were going to starve they'd rather
do it at home.'

They hankered after their families and their villages, with
the camp fires and the palavers, and who could blame them?
If their stomachs were half empty into the bargain, there
was no hope of keeping them in Yalisombo. And if there was
no segregation and no regular treatment leprosy would go on
spreading in the Congo, and who could foretell what the end
would be? So Stanley had gone to see the local administrator
who, as usual, listened to him sympathetically.

'Food,' he said reflectively. 'Food! They're not the only
ones with difficulties over food in these days!' He shook his
head. 'There's a war on! But I understand your problem.
You've been doing an excellent job, and we must help you.
Now, let me see, what would be needed?' He started
enumerating the basic requirements.

'Plantain. Must have plantain. I'll get the village chiefs
and headmen together and persuade them to keep back some

137

of the plantain they take in to the market in Stanleyville each week. They can sell it to you at a reasonable price.

'Palm oil. I'll tell you what we'll do about the palm oil. I'll have a forty-gallon drum delivered to you as soon as you're ready to re-open the leprosarium.

'Meat. Must make sure they have meat. I'll see to it that the local villages provide you with a supply of smoked monkey meat.' He paused a moment, then continued, 'And what about elephant meat? Yes, your patients shall have some elephant meat. I will give the permission. I'll appoint a hunter to kill an elephant once a quarter for the leprosarium at Yalisombo!' This was an unexpected concession for elephants were strictly protected and anyone hunting them without permission was a lawbreaker, liable to a heavy penalty. Armed with these assurances of a better food supply at Yalisombo Stanley had set about persuading the leprosy patients to return. It hadn't proved any easier than before, even with the added inducement of elephant meat, but the place was gradually filling up by the time Raymond Holmes, happily married again, returned from furlough.

A little school had been started in which the teachers themselves were leprosy patients, and Sunday services were now held in a church building of mud bricks topped with a thatched roof. Many a Sunday morning saw Stanley, accompanied by Mali and little Derek, boarding a canoe to cross the mile-wide Congo river to lead the service there.

'We were able to share the good news about Jesus Christ with an increasing number of people who wanted to hear, not only from the leprosy hospital itself, but from the surrounding villages. They got to hear that a white man often preached there and they came to look as well as to listen. When they went home they often retold to their fellow-villagers the sermon they had heard, so the Gospel was spread.

'At that time, I must confess, patients were separated into a special section of the church, apart from the rest of us. We still regarded them as being contagious so they were not to be in very close proximity with those who were healthy.' He himself was prepared to take the risks all doctors and nurses must take when treating people with infectious or contagious diseases, but he was adamant that others must be protected. He was as ignorant as anyone else engaged in leprosy work as to the way leprosy was spread, and to what degree it was a danger to the community at large. As for there being any cure for those with the lepromatous variety, he knew of none. By regular and careful treatment the victims might be spared the extreme horrors of ulcerating extremities and suffering could be alleviated, but in the end the disease would cripple them, disfigure them and perhaps blind them. Nothing could be done then but care for them until they died. There were suggestions in some of the medical journals that a new drug had been developed and was to be tried out, but nothing had materialised yet. Like leprosaria scattered thinly in countries all round the world, the one at Yalisombo could hold out no promise of a permanent cure. The patients in it were free to come and free to go, but in any case they would carry their leprosy with them for life.

*   *   *

The tide of the Second World War had turned at last. The Allied forces were penetrating farther and farther into Europe, and the threat of an Axis invasion into the Belgian Congo was long since over. There was no more talk in Yakusu of hasty evacuations in the Red Devil or any other vehicle that could be mustered. Instead, furloughs were in the air, and in December 1944 Stanley and Mali set off for England. The journey took six weeks, for shipping was scarce and slow, but they arrived safely having encountered nothing more serious than a few false alarms.

They went straight to Mali's parents in Sutton, and made their home with them during the year they were on furlough. The house was large enough to accommodate them comfortably, in a pleasant residential district and within easy reach of London. Stanley travelled widely to address meetings, which varied from small gatherings in country chapels to crowded city churches. It was noticeable that he viewed them all alike. The responsibility and privilege of proclamation was one of his favourite themes, and he accepted without discrimination the invitations that came to him.

A challenging speaker, he prepared his talks and sermons as carefully as the lectures he gave to medical students. He drew freely on his experiences in the Congo, not relating them for their sensational value, but selecting incidents that would illustrate the message he wanted to drive home to his hearers. His retentive memory enabled him to quote aptly from the books he had read, particularly the missionary biographies of pioneers who had been his heroes from boyhood. Speaking out strongly against half-heartedness, he then told of a journey through a rubber plantation in which he noticed a methodical record being made of the amount of latex being produced by each tree. Systematically, impartially, trunk after trunk was tapped, and on the basis of the amount of sap each tree produced, each tree was judged— not by its foliage or the size of its trunk.

> A certain minimum of latex production was set. The tree that was producing more than that minimum was left standing. The tree that was producing only the minimum was spared for a further period of trial. The tree not producing even the minimum amount of the precious latex was ruthlessly cut down. It must go. Not only was it failing in its function, but it was using up nourishment and light and moisture at the expense of the good producers.

> The moral was obvious.

> Is the Master husbandman saying of us 'Why cumbereth it the ground?' Is the axe even now being laid at the root of the tree?

Following up his question with an urgent plea for consecration of talents, means, and the whole life to the service of God, he reminded his hearers of Livingstone's words as he pictured the thousands of African villages where the Gospel of Christ had never been proclaimed—'Anywhere, provided it be forward!' He told them of Harry White who founded a mission centre in the heart of Africa before he died of malaria at the age of thirty-two, and how he had said, 'I must go forward or I go under!'

> We must go forward! I was journeying once up the River Congo in the hospital motor-boat when ahead of us, with bewildering suddenness, three storm centres converged. The wind reached hurricane force, the rain beat down in torrents, all around the waves were black and angry. I knew we were going into a dangerous channel, and asked the African mechanic if we should stop till the storm abated.
> I shall never forget his answer. His eyes looking straight ahead, his hands gripping the wheel, he said,.
> To go back is impossible.
> To stand still is too dangerous.
> We *must* go forward.

Another of his oft-repeated themes was the price to be paid by the disciple of Jesus Christ.

> It may be costly—it often is. No service of value is cheap. It is precisely because so much of our Christian service is formal and half-hearted that we imagine that it is not costly. Privilege carries its responsibilities, and membership of the Church of Christ on earth carries its obligations. It is one thing to be thrilled at the sound of a catchword, and another to sit down quietly and count the cost. The inspiration of a great meeting may fade and vanish, the misplaced romance appertaining to the distant and the unknown soon reveals itself as a hollow mockery. Only as we realise and appropriate for ourselves the constraining love of Christ, catch something of God's tremendous concern for His created beings, can we pay the price.

Many Christians of a former generation were carried away by the watchwords, 'The Congo for Christ', and 'The evangelisation of the world in this generation', but a quiet walk through the 'God's Acre' of any Mission station provides a supplementary and necessary corrective to any superficial enthusiasm.

We need today a combination of scriptural idealism—and a readiness to pay the price. 'I will follow Thee whithersoever Thou goest' must be writ large on our hearts and on our minds. There can be no looking back when we have put our hand to the plough, no specious excuses offered to the Lord of glory when He calls us to service . . .

For Stanley, and perhaps even more for Mali, the price they themselves must pay to follow their Master was becoming increasingly evident and increasingly high as the months of 1945 with the end of World War II slipped off the calendar. It was all centred in the figure of their little son, who became the object of the greatest emotional distress either of them had ever known. No other renunciation could be compared with this. How dear he was to them they had not fully realised until they had to face parting from him.

They had known all along that they must do it, of course. The Mission ruling that no children might be taken back to the Congo still held, and when they left Yakusu they knew they must return there without him. There had never been any question in their minds about it, they knew it was a sacrifice they must make, and they were prepared for it. In theory they approved of the Mission's ruling. The climate of the tropics imposed a physical strain on all white people who went there, and the conditions of the Congo, with its many endemic fevers and diseases to which children were particularly vulnerable made it a dangerous place for them to live in. All down the decades missionaries there had borne the pain of separation from their children as being inextricably bound up in their calling. Their calling! The indefinable awareness that their Master had said to them personally, 'Follow Me', and that for them to do so meant going to the Congo. To a less or greater degree they had all been conscious of it, yet it was here that the conflict arose when natural affections had to be sacrificed.

It arose for Stanley and Mali as the months, then the weeks, then the days of their furlough slipped silently, relentlessly away and they prepared to return to Yakusu, leaving Derek, not yet four years old, behind in England. There was no alternative if they were to fulfil their commission.

They tried to assure themselves that for Derek the separation would mean little, for children were resilient and adaptable, and did not feel these things deeply. A few tears at bedtime, quickly dried as Granny comforted him with the promise of a special treat the next day, and he'd be sleeping peacefully. Mali's parents willingly made themselves responsible for him, there were relatives and friends all eager to give the little boy a good home during the holidays. A suitable school had been found, where the children of missionaries were specially welcomed, where he would have companions of his own age. They told each other it was really going to be much better for him, he needed other children, it was very lonely for him being the only one.

They told him about it, too. Lots of other little boys and girls to play with, Derek, won't that be lovely? You'll be able to share your toys with them, and you'll play with their toys, too! And there will be letters coming, addressed to you. Not many little boys get letters with stamps on coming through the letter-box, but you will. Mummy and Daddy will write you lots of letters . . .

December came with its shortening days, grey skies, sleet, wind, snow. Trunks were brought out, piles of clothes littered the bedroom, books, pots and pans, some new china . . . Some of the clothes Derek had grown out of, too. They'd be needed again in a few months' time, out there in Yakusu . . . Oh, Derek, Derek!

Inevitably there were those who disapproved of the sacrifice they were making.

'Do you feel it's right to go and leave him, so young?'

'Poor little fellow—how can they do it?'

'Putting the work before your own child! I'm sure God doesn't expect that of you!'

How explain that they knew they must endure the ultimate test, as Abraham when he bound Isaac to the altar? How convey to others the inescapable relevance of the Master's words, 'He that loveth . . . son or daughter more than Me is not worthy of Me?' Above all, how communicate to anyone else that which was beyond expression—the silent, strengthening understanding of the God Who so loved the world that He gave His Own Son?

They might have decided to remain at home, leave the Mission, settle in a practice, make a home for their little boy. But they knew they could not do it. Their vows were upon them, and they must go forward.

The day of departure came, and trying to smile they waved goodbye to Derek, firmly clasped in his grandfather's arms. They boarded the ship, settled in their cabin, went along to meals, entered into the routine of ship life. Stanley spent most of his time at a desk in the writing room, going over his notes and his books, studying. Mali sat and knitted or wrote letters, chatting affably to other passengers, listening to their confidences, readily given to one with a sympathetic manner. They spoke little to each other when they were alone together. They didn't mention Derek. When night had fallen, and the other passengers were dancing in the ballroom, or drinking in the bar, or strolling in the moonlight on the deck, they made their way down to their cabin in the Tourists' Class, swaying along the narrow gangway to the motion of the ship, and silently prepared for bed.

'Goodnight, Stanley,' said Mali, slipping between the sheets in the lower bunk.

'Goodnight, dear,' said Stanley, climbing up the little

wooden ladder to the bunk above her. 'Shall I turn off the light?'

'Yes, please.'

Semi-darkness, with tiny chinks of light from the gangway stealing through the slats above the cabin door, a dim translucence from the porthole. The slapping of waves on the side of the ship, distant music from the deck above, the creaking of the partitions, the occasional step of another passenger passing along the gangway. The gentle roll of the ship, the throb of the engine, the screw. Solitude at last, and with it the memories and the longings that had been held at bay in the presence both of sympathetic friends and superficially interested strangers.

A little fair-haired boy, earnestly pulling a toy behind him up the garden steps . . . Chattering . . . Laughing . . . Falling over . . . Crying instinctively for Mummy . . . Running to the door to meet Daddy . . .

Walking along beside that sturdy little figure, hand in hand. Oh, for the feel of that soft little hand!

Stanley heard a sound in the bunk below. It was Mali, trying to muffle the sobs that could be restrained no longer.

He made no effort to comfort her. How could he? He was crying, too.

I wish that the advocates of sexual 'freedom' so-called—not yet discredited in this country by the obvious and appalling necessary corollaries of the views they promulgated in the inter-war years—could catch a glimpse of the uninhibited, unbridled exercise of lust as seen in some primitive African communities. Admittedly, some tribes have strict moral codes, but in others the absence of all restraint, individual and communal, inevitably engenders a variety of deplorable results that stamp themselves on every aspect of family life.

Let us face this dilemma squarely and fearlessly, wherever we happen to be, and unashamedly take our stand for the positive blessings of clean minds and clean bodies; for the unassailable superiority, social and economic and psychological, of 'one man, one wife'; and for the joy and sanctity of life-long unions.

S.G.B.
May 1962
(*From* Some Ethical Dilemmas of a Jungle Doctor
Published by Tyndale Press for C.M.F.)

CHAPTER NINE

Heavy going

One of the things about mud is that it yields. Another thing about it is that it sticks. When the Red Devil carrying Stanley and Mali, their second baby and his nurse, as well as the local *infirmier*, encountered mud, the mud unresistingly received it. Then it clung. Stanley had been driving towards the river at the rate of a couple of miles an hour when the vehicle skidded and came to an obstinate standstill in a gully three feet deep. It took the entire resident population of a village, men, women and children, dragging and shoving, shouting and screaming, to heave it out and set it on its way. When it eventually reached the river, the Red Devil had to be left there, since the five canoes supporting a platform which comprised the ferry had been smashed by the last lorry to use it, so it was out of action. The medical team, liberally splattered with slimy soil, proceeded in a canoe, clearly behind schedule.

Mud was only one of the disadvantages of living in the tropics, a dreary, depressing foe, but not a deadly one. At least it was visible, not like the white ants that gnawed away inside timber until the sudden collapse of what it was supporting revealed the devastation they had wrought. That nearly happened in the second storey of the hospital at Yakusu which contained the main classroom and offices. The providential discovery by some workmen that the timbers supporting it had been eaten hollow forestalled what could have been a terrible disaster. The whole area had to be emptied, causing even more congestion elsewhere and emphasising afresh the urgent need of the new buildings that Holmes and Stanley were engaged in erecting.

They hadn't come to the Congo expecting to turn their hands to brick-making and brick-laying. Those supple, sensitive hands had to be protected and preserved as much as possible for their delicate, intricate work on human bodies. To the surgeon his hands are as important as the musician's are to him. For Stanley particularly the skill of the surgeon was something he would naturally have striven to cultivate and increase, for he had shown unusual ability in the operating theatre, and he knew that the use to which his hands were put could affect that skill.

The matter of using them for brick-laying had arisen out of the discussion he and Holmes had had as to how the main hospital building was actually to be rebuilt. It was essential to rebuild it, and the preliminaries had all been dealt with. All had gone well up to that point. The site was suitable, the Belgian authorities viewed with favour the extension of the B.M.S. hospital and training school in Yakusu, and a grateful Italian patient had drawn up plans which, having been duly studied by the Home Board in London, were approved and passed. Approval and enthusiasm for the scheme from all the right quarters, however, left one vitally important element still lacking. There was no money to pay for it.

Prayer and discussion about it produced no miraculous financial windfall. Instead, the principle that was impressed upon them was along the lines of the practical exhortation, 'Let not thine hands be slack'!

They must raise the money themselves, they decided, and the way to do it would be to increase their medical practice, charging higher fees for consultations and company work. Just at that time the Bamboli Company, which owned several large plantations and was still waiting to appoint a doctor of its own, wanted to extend the Mission's contract, and this timing was providential. The medical service rendered naturally involved more work and travelling, but it also provided some funds on which to draw for materials for the building.

Money for materials – but not enough to pay a professional builder to come and get the job done. Holmes and Stanley looked at each other, then Holmes said,

'Could we manage it ourselves?'

Stanley nodded. 'We could try!'

So that was what they did. They got some expert advice, studied builders' instructions, ordered tons of cement, engaged some workmen, and started building. They made and baked their own bricks in kilns. They sawed their own timber in the forest. They had to do everything.

It was slow-going. The doctors had little time to oversee the workmen, with the consequence that if they each laid as many as seventy-five bricks a day they thought they had done all that could be required of them. 'At this rate we'll still be building a year from now!' Stanley exclaimed. The work was often held up by a deluge of rain which threatened to disperse the cement, anyway, and if building were done in a desultory fashion even in dry weather it could continue indefinitely. It was at this point he decided to take a hand and show what could be achieved. During the rest period in the heat of the day, from noon till two p.m. he went over to the site and, rather stern-faced, laid bricks.

(*Bonganga*, a white man and a doctor, laying bricks!)

When he had proved that he could lay one hundred and fifty bricks in two hours and then go over to the hospital and continue his own day's work as usual, the new building went ahead rather more quickly. His example left the medical students with little excuse to refuse to put in a day's work laying a section of the concrete floor, either. One or two of them weren't too happy about doing it, saying they'd come to learn medicine not haul cement, but most of them worked willingly enough, even when they grumbled.

'*Bonganga*'s a terrible slave-driver,' they said, but admitted that if he drove them he drove himself even harder. The day ended happily with Mali inviting them all to a feast of rice, palm-oil and the delicacy they smacked their lips over—horse-flesh that looked like corned beef but tasted even better.

It was about this time that news of a visit to Yakusu being planned for the Prince of the Belgians put the place in a titter of excitement. A Royal visitor! Paths were re-gravelled, weeds plucked out, grass cut, flowering plants appeared in boxes all over the place, needlewomen were kept busy on a huge banner with the words *Vive le Prince Régent*. Flags were produced, an awning made, and the wife of the senior missionary brought out her best china and daintiest table-cloths, and wondered what she could give His Royal Highness for tea.

When the great day dawned, hours before the royal steamer was due to arrive, the entire population of Yakusu was down on the waterfront, dressed in their best, the younger schoolchildren with brightly coloured paper skirts specially made for the occasion. Everything was colourful and animated and cheerful—except the weather. The weather was in a very bad mood. After several days of brilliant sunshine clouds now darkened the sky, the wind howled, the water surged grey and sullen, then the rain gushed down, obliterating the low green banks on the other side of the river. The drums announced the approach of the Prince's steamer, but the storm was so fierce it was impossible for it to anchor, and there it was, bobbing up and down on the angry waters while the people of Yakusu stood wet and bedraggled on what had been clean, well-swept beaches and roads, but was now just a sea of mud.

Thick mud.

Even if the storm abated sufficiently for him to get into the mission launch and be brought ashore, wouldn't His Royal Highness baulk at the mud? Wouldn't he decide that the only thing to do was to give up the visit and return to Stanleyville, and perhaps come to Yakusu some other time? Spirits drooped damply, like the flags and the awning and the banner.

But it is required of a prince that he be a good sport, and so Prince Charles of the Belgians proved to be. He flatly refused to go back to Stanleyville, and after an hour or so, when the fierce elements had turned merely sulky, he came ashore and stood at attention, loftily indifferent to the rain, while everyone sang the Belgian National Anthem. Then he saluted, bowed gracefully, waved aside a proffered mackintosh, walked through the mud with royal contempt, and when it was suggested that in the circumstances he might prefer to cut out some of the programme, he would have none of it.

'Certainly not,' he said. 'I want to see everything. Bah! I've been in much worse weather than this in the navy!'

He was escorted round the school, introduced to the Mission staff and the six African pastors, taken to the hospital and into the medical school, then came to a halt before something that obviously gripped his attention. On the walls were maps of the Belgian Congo, and on the maps were little coloured pins, not only in the main villages but also scattered widely in rural areas, on plantations, deep in the forests. He looked at them enquiringly.

'What are these?' he enquired.

Stanley was prompt to explain. He had made the maps himself, working on them with his usual meticulous care. They represented what was the most valuable and far-reaching contribution the B.M.S. doctors were making to the health of the Belgian Congo.

'These coloured pins represent the *infirmiers* who have been trained here in the Medical School,' he said. 'These are the places where they are working. Over here in the east of the Congo, helping the doctors fighting plague . . . in a lab. dissecting malaria-carrying mosquitoes . . . In Stanleyville hospital, in charge of the operating theatre . . .

'And these are the *infirmiers* working in the districts for which we are responsible,' he continued, rapidly circling the area of ten thousand square miles in the midst of which Yakusu lay. 'We've got fourteen rural dispensaries here, you'll notice. Each dispensary has four or five clinics to which the *infirmiers* travel regularly. Those boys are doing a fine job. We're proud of them. I marvel sometimes at the skill and ingenuity they display. Only last week I met an *infirmier* who had sewed up a little boy's abdomen. He had fallen from a tree, and actually walked to the dispensary holding loops of intestine in his hand.'

'What did he use for stitches?' asked the prince.

'He made his own sutures from palm-frond fibre and sterilised them. He has initiative, that boy.' Stanley moved on.

'This map shows where the *infirmiers* have come from.' The prince's eye ranged from north to south, east to west, where more little pins appeared. 'They come from all over the country,' he observed thoughtfully, moving away rather reluctantly. Those maps had evidently made an impression.

Sometime later it was revealed that he had inaugurated, with a handsome donation, the Congo Welfare Fund, which was used for helping to improve the conditions of people living in rural areas.

The following year Stanley, to his surprise, received a letter from the Provincial Governor telling him that he was to be honoured publicly for his services in the Belgian Congo. It was the first decoration he received—*Chevalier de l'Ordre Royal du Lion*.

The outward encouragements and successes were not unattended by afflictions, however. It was heartening to have the new hospital nearing completion, to see the progress being made in the training of the medical auxiliaries, to go Sunday by Sunday to a packed church, to know of a steady stream of men, women and young people who were taking their stand as Christians. The big mission centre at Yakusu was a happy place to work in, and the Brownes' bungalow with its verandah facing across the wide expanse of the Congo River a happy home to return to every evening, with another little child, Alastair, to bath and put to bed instead of Derek. Yes, it was a happy home, yet for both Stanley and Mali it was not perfectly so, because Derek was not there. As with all normal parents, each child had his own unique place in their affections, that no one else could fill, and the presence of their second and then their third-born sons could not entirely assuage the longing for their absent first-born. The acute pain at the separation had settled into a sort of semi-conscious ache that could be hidden and endured, however, when a letter arrived which pierced like a knife and set the emotions throbbing again.

It was from Mali's parents, and it told them as gently as possible that Derek had been very unhappy. The school into which he had been put with such high hopes had certainly not suited him, due mainly to what is known as a personality clash between him and the matron. For some reason not defined he did not like her and she, it appeared, did not like him. Whatever means she had employed to enforce her will upon him had proved singularly unsuccessful, for the little boy, in self-defence, had simply refused to eat. When the Rev. and Mrs. Williamson had gone on a Saturday afternoon to visit him they were so shocked at the change in him that they had removed him from the school then and there, and brought him home with them. He was much better now, and his appetite was returning, they assured his parents, but of course another school would have to be found, and it would take a little while for the child to get over what had been a very disturbing experience.

There was nothing they could do about it. The natural instinct to drop everything and fly to his relief had to be denied, for as they talked and prayed together about it one thing emerged of which they were both aware. It was God's will for them to be there in Yakusu. The hundreds of people in the forest and rural areas whose very lives could be at stake if they were deprived of Stanley's medical skills provided one unescapable reason for remaining. Besides, they were an integral part of the missionary team at Yakusu and to leave suddenly would be to let the others down. They must stay where they were, knowing that Derek's grandparents would do as much for him as they could do themselves. But the grief and anxiety over their little boy, and the desire to be with him and comfort him, were very strong, casting a shadow for many weeks, until they knew he was himself again, and happily settled into another school.

A different kind of anxiety, particularly for Stanley, was concerned with the leprosarium at Yalisombo. Some trouble or other seemed constantly to be flaring up there, with quarrels among the patients, grumbling about the food, and numbers fluctuating as in ones or twos, sometimes in groups, the disgruntled took themselves off back to their own villages, refusing to remain any longer in what was to them an artificial and unnatural environment. Useless to remonstrate with them, point out that the debilitating effects of the disease made them an easy prey to all the other physical ills they would meet with away from the careful protection afforded at Yalisombo. 'If I'm going to die, I'll die,' was the fatalistic attitude, 'I'd rather die at home. You can't cure me, so why should I stay?'

It was a depressing business, and Stanley felt sometimes that they were getting nowhere with their fight against the disease.

It was even more depressing when they had to admit as a patient the most brilliant *infirmier* ever to pass through the Yakusu Medical School, Dickie, Richard Likoso.

The day when Stanley stood on the shore watching Dickie and his family being rowed across the river towards Yalisombo was one of the saddest in his life. There was an unusually close relationship between him and Dickie, for although their origins were so widely separated, their basic experiences were very similar.

Like Stanley, Dickie came from an obscure background, for he was a member of the Heso, a small tribe situated in a remote area. Like Stanley he had a Christian home, for his father had been the first in his village to turn from spirit worship to serve the living and true God. To take such a stand had demanded both courage and conviction and

Dickie, as a lad, had sturdily embraced the faith of his father.

The similarity in experience continued, for Dickie too had to work for his living. He went to school, earning the money needed to pay for his tuition by acting as house-boy to a pioneer missionary couple. It was here Stanley first met him. 'A most delightful boy, serving most graciously at table,' was the way he described him. 'They told me they had never had a student like him, he was top in every subject in his year.'

Later on he was admitted to Yakusu, in the first year of the school for the training of medical auxiliaries, and here too, by a combination of inherent ability and diligent work, he soared to the top.

'He managed to get first place in every subject, including vocabulary, and in those days the vocabulary concentrated on Lokele and French. In spite of Lokele being a foreign language for him, he came top in this examination, too. Throughout the three years of his medical course there was no more efficient, helpful, industrious and competent student than he.'

He was, in fact, a young man after Stanley's own heart, and a bond was forged between them which persisted through the years when Dickie completed his medical training by doing practical work in the dispensaries and the leprosarium, married a charming young Christian who had trained as a pupil midwife at Yakusu, and set off with her to man a dispensary in the far north-east of the country, a thousand miles away, near the border of Sudan. It was a government appointment, but letters continued to pass between teacher and pupil.

'Then I detected a little note of distress, of uncertainty, in one of his letters. He had pins and needles in the little finger of one hand and on the adjacent side of the ring finger. He said it wasn't very much but it persisted and he could not understand it.' He could not understand it, but Stanley knew what he was thinking, and acted promptly, as usual.

'Come as soon as you can,' he wrote, 'and we'll give you a thorough examination,' Dickie obtained the necessary permission to take a short leave, and came to Yakusu.

Stanley could find nothing wrong with him. His skin was clear, the numbness and the tingling had gone, blood and urine tests, nasal smears and skin scrapings were all negative.

'Everything's all right, Dickie,' he said. 'It's just a touch of "imaginitis",' he added laughing. 'One of the diseases of Western civilisation, not often found among Africans.' So Dickie went back the three days' journey on a lorry, and settled down to his work again. He sent Stanley reports of what he was doing, the surveys for yaws and sleeping sickness and tuberculosis, the clinics he was opening, the growth of the local churches (he was in a region where the Africa Inland Mission was working), of the preaching he did, in the local language, too, for Dickie's gifts included those of the linguist.

Then came another letter. The pins and needles had come back again, and they persisted. He wasn't feeling too well, had a slight fever. It was nearly time for his vacation, and he'd like to come to Yakusu for *Bonganga* to give him another medical overhaul.

This time he arrived surprisingly quickly, bringing with him his wife and their two little daughters. The tests started again. Stanley was slightly puzzled. There was nothing wrong with Dickie's skin, no leprous patches, his nerves seemed normal, blood tests proved negative. 'Now we'll take a nasal smear, stain it with Ziehl Neelsen and see if we can find what we hope we won't find.' He obtained a little discharge from Dickie's nose, and when alone, stained it, peering anxiously through the microscope. Nothing there. He stained another smear. Nothing there. He found Dickie and told him, 'I've looked through many stained slides, and I've found nothing at all suggestive of leprosy. You're clear, Dickie,' he said, and Dickie's face broadened into a wide smile. But some instinct still warned him all was not well.

'*Bonganga*,' he said rather diffidently. 'Will you take one more slide? Will you examine the nasal mucosa? There might be something hidden away there, mightn't there?'

It was the final test, and there was not the slightest evidence from all the others that any leprosy bacilli were lurking in that strong, healthy-looking body. It seemed unnecessary, but Stanley agreed. He took a scraping from the lining of Dickie's nostril, and immediately made a slide, fixed it, stained it, then peered through the microscope, confident everything would be as with all the others.

Slowly he focussed on area after area, glad that he'd be able to convince Dickie that all his haunting fears must be dispelled when suddenly he caught his breath. What was that? His eye had seen something red.

Hating what he saw, peering more intently through the microscope, he stared at them—a clump of those evil, rod-like little red bacilli, the *Mycobacterium leprae* that had defied medical science all down the years, and still remained triumphant. And because he was learning to discern the various characteristics of the disease and the degrees of resistance to it in the cells of the body, he knew that the clumping together in one little cell that he saw through his ally, the microscope, denoted what was most to be feared. Dickie had really got leprosy—and not the indeterminate leprosy, the mere transient skin patch that would heal itself. He hadn't even got tuberculoid leprosy, affecting the appearance of the skin permanently and eventually destroying the nerves. That would have been bad, but with good food and careful treatment he could have gone on living a normal life. But that clumping together of the red bacilli, like a band of guerillas hidden but ready to strike secretly at the unwary, meant only one thing. What Dickie had in his body was 'the mother of the bad leprosy'.

How could he tell him? How let him know that his deep-seated intuitive fear had proved correct?

'You were right about that mucosa test,' he said as casually as possible. 'There was something there, after all. You'll have to stay here for a bit while we look after you.' There was no need to say much more. Dickie understood. The expression on his face told him that.

'He knew what it meant. Going to Yalisombo. Watching his disease getting worse in spite of those painful injections of chaulmoogra oil. Feeling his nerves become tender and enlarged. Sensation disappearing from his extremities. Ulceration, disfigurement. Deformity. Blindness perhaps . . . Uselessness . . .'

When Stanley went to tell Mr. Ennals, the senior missionary, what he had seen through the microscope, the expression on his face was the same as that on Dickie's own.

*   *   *

Pastor Lititiyo ascended the steps of the Brownes' little bungalow rather slowly, for he was getting on in years and a bit stiff at the joints. Stanley was at his desk, the place he was usually to be found when at home, and rose with a smile when he saw his visitor. The two of them understood each other well. Their association had started at the time Stanley arrived in Yakusu, a raw young missionary whose unwitting mistakes in speaking the local language had often been corrected wisely by the old ex-cannibal. Ex-cannibal, Lititiyo undoubtedly was, having met his first missionary when returning triumphantly from a little foray with a neighbouring tribe, the juicy thigh of a slain enemy tucked under his arm.

The missionary was quite short, not at all the sort of fellow to tackle a cannibal, but he had stood his ground, stopping Lititiyo in his tracks and remonstrating fearlessly with him. Millman was his name. He came from Leicester, where he had been a school teacher before he joined the B.M.S., which had perhaps given him a certain authority when it came to dealing with teenagers. Also, he was very sure of his commission to preach the Gospel to everyone, and that included cannibals. The outcome of that strange encounter was that Lititiyo, to the surprise and indignation of his fellow-tribesmen, listened to the teaching of the white man who had come into their midst, was convinced of the truth of it, and declared he intended to be a follower of the God, Jesus Christ, come what may. Some forty-odd years later he was senior pastor of all the Baptist churches in Yakusu district, a sort of patriarchal figure among them, esteemed by all. At the annual conferences for church leaders he took his place as the chairman, and it was in this capacity he had come to see Stanley. The annual conference was in session, and it was customary for one of the missionary doctors to be asked to speak about some aspect of the medical work they were doing. On this occasion it was *Bonganga* Browne's turn, and the pastor had come to talk to him about it.

'Yes, certainly I'll come along tomorrow and give you a talk,' said Stanley obligingly. 'What do you want me to speak about?'

'Leprosy.'

'Leprosy?' Stanley was surprised and somewhat nettled. The leprosy work was at a very low ebb indeed. As everyone knew, the latest crisis at the leprosarium at Yalisombo had been one of the worst, and had resulted in the place being nearly emptied again. Even Dickie's gracious and inspiring presence had failed to restrain his discontented and despondent fellow-sufferers from departing.

'Yes, leprosy,' persisted Pastor Lititiyo, 'and what you are going to do about it.'

'What am I going to do about it? I'm not going to do anything about it!' replied Stanley, rather tartly. He was fed up with leprosy! 'We've tried twice and we've failed twice. You remember how all the people at Yalisombo went away because they weren't getting enough food, and how we got good food supplies for them. And now they've gone away again because they don't like the medicine we're giving them. Well, we haven't got any other medicine, so what else can we do? We've done our best, and we've failed.'

The old pastor looked at him silently, and Stanley continued,

'We've got plenty of other work to do. There's this busy hospital with fifteen to twenty operations every week, and often only one doctor here to do them. There's the teaching in the school for medical auxiliaries, and now that the whole district is being opened up, ten thousand square miles of jungle with all the people in it needing to be treated and helped . . . And what with epidemics flaring up, and yaws and tuberculosis and malaria and everything else, we've got enough to do without thinking any more about leprosy!'

But even as he said it, he knew it was wrong. He could not dismiss the subject just like that. However apparently fruitless all their efforts had proved, however ungrateful the victims of the disease had shown themselves, they could not be abandoned, nor could the disease be ignored. It was not only the biggest medical problem in the district now. It presented a social, even a spiritual challenge which was not being faced.

'All right,' said Stanley after a short pause. 'I'll come with you tomorrow and talk to the church leaders—about leprosy, and what we're going to do about it.'

There was something very significant about the timing of that church leaders' annual conference in Yakusu, and particularly the meeting which Stanley had had forced upon him. He was very moved as he spoke, admitting their medical impotence to do much for the leprosy sufferers. 'We've tried. We missionaries opened the leprosarium, but we've achieved very little. There is not the medicine to heal this disease. We've had the medicine for sleeping sickness, and malaria, and yaws, and even for smallpox—but not for leprosy. There have been one or two references in some American magazines and pamphlets I get to a new drug that may prove effective, but that's all I can say. We still haven't got anything to cure leprosy.

'Meanwhile, it's over to you. Yes, to *you*. All we doctors have been able to do has been to show love and compassion in Christ's Name. Maybe that's all you can do, you Christian leaders, but what about doing it? What about some of you men going into the forest and clearing ground for new gardens for those men who can't cut the forest any more because their hands and their feet are ulcerated? What about some of you women helping to plant the rice and the peanuts and the maize? What about helping with their cooking the women whose hands are ulcerated?

'You ask what I'm going to do about leprosy. I ask what are *we* going to do about leprosy. We're faced with a problem that is not only physical. It's social and spiritual as well, and we must face it together, all of us. We can't ignore the plight of these people, push them out. That's not Christ's way. We'll be failing Him if we don't do something practical to help them—and show them love while we're doing it, too!'

He made his point clear. The church leaders' meeting turned into a prayer meeting, as one after another they acknowledged their previous hardness of heart towards people suffering from leprosy, and resolved to do what they could to help them now. A new and more personal concern had been born in the hearts of the leaders in the little churches scattered throughout the whole district, preparing the way for the miracle through medicine that was even now travelling towards them.

Before they call I will answer; and while they are yet speaking I will hear.

The prayers that ascended that morning in Yakusu for the people with leprosy were a case in point, for even as they were praying a little parcel addressed to Dr. Stanley Browne in Yakusu, Belgian Congo, was lying in a sack of mail en route to Stanleyville. A few hours later he received a chit from the Post Office there, notifying him of the arrival of a small box from America, awaiting collection. He had no idea what it contained. He signed the chit and sent it back in the usual way, and two or three days later the parcel was delivered to Yakusu.

'I can see it now, a little round box, accompanied by some literature, sent by the American Mission to Lepers. It explained that this was a new drug, produced by an American firm. It had been tried out in Carville, Louisiana, and had given good results in leprosy. So here was a sample, and I was asked to try it out on the African form of leprosy, to see if it could be given with safety and good effect to the patients they knew I was interested in.'

It had come! No longer was it confined to laboratories where research chemists worked quietly and steadily through the years. It had actually been tried out with success, and was now being sent to French Indo-China, South-East Asia, South America—and among other places, to Central Africa, to be tried out in Yakusu.

He and Holmes and Trevor Knights, who had rejoined them, studied the literature carefully. The compound was called Diasone (a derivative of dapsone). The possible side effects were nausea, vomiting, diarrhoea, skin rashes, blood dyscrasia, etc.

They discussed it all with mixed feelings, of hope and apprehension.

'We'll need some human guinea pigs. We'll have to explain the possibility of these side effects to them. We mustn't over-persuade anyone—they've got to volunteer willingly to try the new medicine.'

They wondered if volunteers would be forthcoming. The best one for it would be Dickie, they knew. With his intelligence, his medical knowledge and experience, he would understand what was going on, be quick to recognise the effects of the drug upon himself. But he would also be aware of the danger inherent in any such trial, that the drug, instead of healing, might even increase his pain and shorten his life. They knew they couldn't ask it of him, yet without testing out the drug there would be no way of discovering its efficacy, no way of releasing the means of healing. The three men bowed their heads in prayer.

The following day Stanley and Mali boarded a canoe and were paddled the half-hour journey to Yalisombo. Everything took its usual course for the weekly visit of *Bonganga*. Up the steep bank to the little dispensary where the patients were gathered round the steps, the hymn singing followed by a short reading from the Bible and a brief exposition, prayer, and then,

'I've got some good news for you today,' said Stanley. 'I've brought with me a new medicine. We hope it's going to cure leprosy.' He looked round and sensed at once the unbelief, the scorn.

'A medicine to heal leprosy!' the murmur went round, 'Everybody knows nothing can cure leprosy. Once the ulcers come there's nothing you can put on them that does any good. Leprosy isn't an ordinary disease—it's different. There's no medicine that will cure leprosy.'

'Well, we'll never know unless we try,' said Stanley. 'It was sent from America, and we're told it has proved successful in a hospital there. I know there's a risk, taking a medicine that we haven't tried out here, but we can only try it out on someone who's got leprosy. Isn't there anyone here who's willing to take the risk, for the sake of others as well as himself?'

Only one hand went up. It was Dickie's.

'I'm willing,' he said. The disease was progressing rapidly in him. He had patches all over his body, pain in the external popliteal nerve, and the beginning of a right foot drop. 'I've got nothing to lose. You can try it out on me.'

In the light of fundamental Christian principles, the ruthless and unthinking disruption of the ecological balance cannot but be wrong, whatever the immediate benefits. It may appear, anthropocentrically speaking, as if the earth might have been specifically designed for the exclusive use of twentieth-century so-called civilised Man. He has acquired the technology, the know-how, the instrumentation, the intellectual apparatus to enable him to investigate, and exploit, and utilise. But, apart from a realisation of his accountability to God, he is helpless before his own technology.

S.G.B.

(At an address given at the Annual Breakfast of the Christian Medical Fellowship on Tuesday 27 July 1971 during the British Medical Association's Annual Meeting at Leicester)

CHAPTER TEN

End of a chapter

Raymond Holmes had resigned. Stanley heard of it one night early in 1950, at the end of a journey in the Red Devil during which he had driven one hundred and fifty muddy miles without brakes. The news came as a heavy blow. Not only did it mean he would be left practically single-handed again, but it meant the break-up of a partnership which had been of unusual closeness. The two of them had accomplished so much together, seen eye to eye on all vital matters, relied on each other unquestioningly, commiserated together over medical setbacks, rejoiced over successes. Holmes had been there in the early days of the leprosy breakthrough, when Dickie had offered to be the human guinea pig for the new drugs, and they'd talked and prayed, together with Trevor Knights, about the dose they should give him. One tablet a day—three tablets a day, trying them out cautiously, watching for reactions in the blood and kidneys particularly, asking anxiously when Dickie's face swelled and he suffered acute discomfort of a lepra reaction, 'Shall we stop, Dickie? Have you had enough?' They'd caught each other's eye when he answered, 'No, go ahead. I can take it,' shared the sense of responsibility as they took him at his word. Then they'd seen the effect of the drugs on those evil little red bacilli at the fortnightly examinations, observed them gradually breaking up, sensed the tension of alternating hope and disappointment in the leprosarium, then the slow upsurge of excitement as it became obvious to everyone that Dickie was getting better. The patches on his skin were repigmenting, his ears were losing their thickened appearance . . . the white man's new medicine was actually curing Dickie's leprosy.

Then Holmes and his wife left for furlough. When they returned it would be the Brownes' turn, and after that the Trevor Knights'. Everything appeared to be going smoothly until word came that Irene Holmes's health was not good, and their return must be delayed for a few weeks. And now this! Irene had had a serious operation, her condition wouldn't allow for a return to the Congo, so there was nothing else for it but for him to resign.

For Stanley it not only meant that his own furlough must be cut short if he were to get back in time for Trevor Knights to go on his. It marked the end of an era, though he did not realise it at the time. Imperceptibly but irrevocably the old order was changing. The stern simplicity of the days when central Africa was in the backwoods, and the missionary lived there in almost total isolation was giving way to the more complicated influences of the post-war period. The motor-boat was taking the place of the canoe, the aeroplane of the river-steamer. Better roads were making travelling easier, while industry provided Africans coming out of the bush with the opportunity of earning quick money in the townships—and Western civilisation was not slow to provide quick ways of spending it. And if the witch-doctors retained, to a great extent, their hold over superstitious villagers, they did so dressed in European clothes rather than skins and feathers. All this had its effect on missionary life. Raymond Holmes's resignation was a landmark in the transition from one to the other.

As in all the colonial countries of Africa during that new decade, political forces were at work which were eventually to overthrow the old regime and usher in a new one. Anti-white feelings were mounting to such an extent that in the late fifties the Belgian colonial government advised that in the province of which Stanleyville was the capital white drivers should not attempt to go to the help of villagers injured or killed on the road. The reason for this was that when trying to help victims of an accident some drivers had been severely beaten up, or even killed out of hand by angry Africans who knew nothing of the cause of the accident.

Rumours were rife. One of these was that a red lorry was touring the country, capturing people and canning them as corned beef. A Belgian doctor in charge of a chain of dispensaries on the south bank of the Congo opposite Yakusu heard the rumour, and thought of the *docteurs anglais* driving around in their Red Devil. He knew Stanley well, esteemed his surgical skill so highly that he asked for him to perform a serious operation on his wife, and would have been very sorry indeed if anything had happened to him on the road.

The new decade ushered in, in 1950, was to lead up to all the horrors of the Simba uprising and the disruption of missionary work around Yakusu for years, but no premonition of that clouded the minds of Stanley and Mali as they discussed the immediate implications of the Holmes' retirement and their own furlough. There was no one in view to replace him, few doctors were offering for missionary service, and to leave Trevor Knights alone with the responsibility of the leprosarium as well as all the medical work of hospital and district was too heavy a burden.

On the other hand there was Derek to be considered. It was four years since they had left him—would he even recognise his own parents? As for his two younger brothers, he had never even seen them.

'We must go back—for his sake! And oh, I'm longing to see him . . .'

Eventually they arrived at a compromise. Mali with Alastair and Christopher would go home in time for Derek's Easter holiday, while Stanley would follow in July for a three months' leave, when another doctor would come to Yakusu temporarily. It meant a much shorter furlough than they had expected, but they promised themselves a longer one later on.

Six months later they were back again at Yakusu. During that time Mali had had two operations, and Stanley had been seriously ill with an inflamed liver associated with amoebic dysentery. It had not been much of a holiday for either of them. However, they had seen Derek, knew he was happily settled in his new school, and as the Mission's ruling regarding children in the Congo had been modified, they were spared the anguish of leaving Alastair and Christopher behind. They returned to a situation which was more encouraging than anything they had known before, something that surpassed their most optimistic dreams.

Trevor Knights had carried on practically single-handed, and even in the comparatively short time that Stanley had been absent the medicine that had worked such marvels for Dickie was being tried with equal success on other patients. The tom-toms were drumming the incredible news all over the ten thousand square miles of their medical district and beyond, that people were being healed of leprosy, the really serious kind of leprosy, by means of a wonder drug at Yalisombo.

No difficulty now in persuading patients to come! They came unannounced, many of them, walking, hobbling, some even crawling on all fours, using any possible means to get to the place where at last there was hope. In two years the community that had numbered 118 when Dickie offered to be the first human guinea pig for the new drug, had grown to over a thousand.

What activity now! They've got to live somewhere—up with the wattle-and-daub huts, rows and rows of them! This was something the able-bodied Yakusu Christians could do to help, and they did.

What about bedding? The Government, alert to what was going on, supplied one grey blanket for each patient, and paid the salaries of two more *infirmiers* to help with the treatment and oversight into the bargain.

Food! How shall we feed them? Plant gardens, grow rice and peanuts, extract the oil from the palm-nuts.

And meat! Tell the hospital we need more meat—antelope and monkey as well as the quarterly elephant.

But how to get the money to buy all the drugs that were needed? The grant being received was not sufficient for the people who were flocking to Yalisombo. Letters sent hopefully to the B.M.S. drew hearty good wishes, but no cash. Finances at home were low, it was explained, and offers of service were low, too, scarcely enough to maintain the existing work of the Mission, so it was no use asking for reinforcements for the new and rapidly growing leprosy work. It turned out for good in the end, as more and more responsibility was shouldered by the young *infirmiers*, especially Dickie. As for the money, by increasing his private practice and ploughing all his fees back into the hospital and leprosarium, Stanley managed to obtain enough to buy the drugs needed for all who were admitted into Yalisombo. He had to shelve the thought of the many sufferers who were scattered throughout the vast district assigned to him who were not being treated. He could do nothing for them—not yet. He had stacks of clinical notes about them, knew the villages they lived in, the nearest dispensaries, but without the drugs to begin the long process of destroying those little red bacilli lurking in their bodies, he was powerless to help them. He was like a general with an army strategically deployed but unable to go into action for lack of ammunition.

By this time news of what was happening in Yalisombo was reaching far and wide among the organisations concerned with leprosy, however, and applications to them eventually brought help. One day the news reached him that the American Mission to Lepers was prepared to make a large grant of further supplies of medicine—so large that he knew he could embark on a campaign of war against leprosy throughout the whole district.

So now to action! Out came those bundles of medical notes stacked up in the bungalow. 'We must get out a separate card for everyone in the district known to have leprosy.' Mali wrote out 4,500 cards with the name, age, sex, parentage, village, form of leprosy and nearest dispensary of every patient, Stanley and Dickie making separate records in a register. The next step was to distribute them when he visited the dispensaries (eighteen of them spread over hundreds of miles) and put the position frankly to each of the *infirmiers*.

'We've got the drug that will cure leprosy. Something we've longed for and prayed for and now we've got it. We can really help these people at last. But it's going to be a long, long fight with the disease. It's not like the yaws that can be healed with a few pricks of the needle. You can't be immunised against it with a scratch on the arm, as with smallpox. It's got to be tablets or injections regularly week by week, for months, even years . . . It's going to mean taking smears regularly, checking progress, keeping records.

'You're already doing a full-time job. Can you take on this extra load? See, here are the cards of everyone in your district with leprosy. Fifty of them . . . A hundred of them . . . Two hundred of them . . . It'll be a man-sized job, keeping track of them all. Are you willing for it?'

But they were man-size workers, every one of them. He came back from those visits to the *infirmiers* high in his praise of them. These were the lads he had taught in the school for medical auxiliaries, seen through their exams; whom he had seen not only industriously studying in the classrooms but with heads bowed in the church, heard not only their shouts on the football field but their vows made to God. And now, launched out into arduous and often lonely service, not one of them had demurred at taking on what they knew would be a long and tedious addition to their weekly programme. In many cases their enthusiasm had matched his own, inspiring him afresh.

They were as good as their word, the *infirmiers*, and so were the patients. Dread of the extreme ravages of the disease that all had seen, and desire for healing was so deep and so strong that even the fatalistic, lethargic forest dwellers turned up regularly for their medicine, topping ninety per cent attendance. They were halcyon days, those early years of the 1950s, where the campaign against leprosy was concerned.

Mistakes were made, of course. Drugs were given to all, including the burnt-out cases in whom the bacilli had done their worst and who were no longer suffering from active leprosy. There were setbacks, too. At one stage Dickie again had a tingling sensation in his right leg, numbness and a tender, swollen nerve trunk. It eventually proved to be nothing worse than inflammation caused by dead or dying bacilli in the nerve fibres, which massage and extra vitamins soon put right, but it caused anxiety. Some patients responded to treatment very slowly, and a few proved to be allergic to dapsone, so that little could be done for them. But all in all the introduction of dapsone into the treatment of the disease was a major advance in Yalisombo, as it was in other leprosaria in various parts of the world. Nothing comparable to this had ever happened in the field of leprosy before, and at last there was hope for the victim of leprosy.

*　　*　　*

If Dr. Robert Cochrane had stuck strictly to his assignment, he would probably not have visited Yalisombo at all in 1954. As the newly-appointed Technical Medical Adviser to the American Mission to Lepers Inc. (now American Leprosy Missions Inc.), his task was to visit work being done under their auspices, and an all-British mission like the B.M.S. did not come into that category. The world-famous leprologist was not going to let little things like that deter him from learning more about his subject, however, nor from imparting his encyclopaedic knowledge anywhere it would be put to the best and widest use possible for the ultimate benefit of those suffering from leprosy. He was coming to the end of a two-year survey which had taken him to India, Malaya, Thailand, Northern Nigeria and the French Cameroons when he arrived in the Belgian Congo. If he had not heard of Yalisombo before he could not fail to hear of it now, and he determined to go and see it for himself. When it came to presenting the report of his findings over the period in which he had studied and compared leprosy treatment in various places, he explained his inclusion of Yalisombo in the tour as being a fraternal visit, not an official one.

All the same, the welcome he received in Stanleyville was an unexpectedly official one. Somewhat to his surprise, not only were doctors of the Baptist Missionary Society and the Regions Beyond Missionary Union there to meet him, but several Belgian officials as well, including the Provincial Medical Officer. Arrangements had been made for him to give a lecture on leprosy to all the medical men, nurses and final year *infirmiers* in Stanleyville if he agreed. He grasped the opportunity gladly, noting privately that the Protestant missions seemed to be working in very satisfactory co-operation with the government. This, in Dr. Cochrane's view, was just as it should be. He did not consider it was the function of missions to take over the health programme of the country in which they were working. 'We cannot meet need; we can only show how need can be met,' he was frequently asserting in his consultations with mission leaders, and the training of young Africans, such as he saw at Yakusu, was the way to do it. Reporting later, he observed that many of them went into Government service as committed Christians, 'a fine contribution to the cause of non-professional missionary work'. One way and another, Dr. Cochrane approved of everything he saw of the medical programme in Yakusu.

It was the leprosarium at Yalisombo in particular that he had come to see, however, and his arrival coincided with a very joyful event. One hundred patients there were ready for discharge. The certificates pronouncing them to be cured of leprosy were presented to them in the presence of an august company of officials, including the Belgian District Commissioner. Dr. Cochrane gave the address, with Stanley translating.

By this time the leprosy colony had been beautified with flowering plants and trees, lawns and walks, and the old atmosphere of despair had been replaced by a cheerful spirit that always surprised people visiting it for the first time. 'They seem so happy!' was a frequent ejaculation heard as they walked round. 'I'd expected them to be very sad, but they don't seem like that at all.'

The transformation was inward as well as outward, for a spiritual revival had taken place since those discouraging early years. Until that momentous prayer meeting of the church leaders when Stanley had been asked to speak to them about leprosy, only two patients had come forward for baptism. Since that time, however, a steady stream of people in Yalisombo had been openly confessing their faith in Jesus Christ as their Saviour and Lord. A large church had been built by the patients themselves, most of the materials having been supplied by the members of the Yakusu church. It was not the product of charity from overseas.

'This really is a remarkable institution,' Dr. Cochrane reported, and went on to expatiate not only on the laboratory and dispensary buildings, which he pronounced first-class, but also on the ability of the man whom he recognised as being behind it all. 'He is really brilliant,' he wrote, '. . . and quite modest about it all.' With him in charge, Dr. Cochrane saw Yalisombo as an auxiliary research laboratory linked with fundamental research laboratories abroad. Air travel would make visits rapid and easy. The records for which Dr. Browne was responsible were the best he had seen, he said, and the clinical material was invaluable. All possible encouragement should be given to this unusually gifted and dedicated man in his fight again leprosy, and the more so because he was first and foremost a missionary seeking by every means in his power to extend the Kingdom of God. No one who knew him was left in any doubt about his personal faith and convictions, and this weighed very heavily in his favour where Dr. Cochrane was concerned.

Stanley himself knew nothing of the impression he had made on his illustrious visitor, nor how it was to affect his future career. At the time of Dr. Cochrane's visit he had other matters besides leprosy on his mind, uppermost of which was onchocerciasis, or river blindness as it was called.

River blindness had always been present in the district, but now there were three or four areas where it was becoming serious. The intolerable itching, the thickened ugly skin, the piebald patches on his patients' legs told their own story. The minute parasites that had been injected into the skin of the leg by the low-flying black-fly were silently multiplying, and as they worked their way upwards would eventually blind, even kill, many of their victims.

Something must be done to stop the disease spreading, and drastic action was needed. The scourge must be dealt with at source, as with the tse-tse fly that was the transmitter of sleeping sickness. Stanley decided that he would wage war on the black-fly.

He discussed the matter first with the Belgian Provincial Medical Officer, gained his full approval, and then, as was typical of him, enlisted the co-operation of his *infirmiers* in training. He taught them to take snips of skin from people in whom the parasites were present, let them examine under the microscope the tiny, thread-like worms, told them how they got there, enthused them with the desire that was gripping him.

'These are the parasites that make people go blind, as they work their way up into the eyes,' he explained. 'They're carried by the black-fly that is found by the rivers and streams. Eliminate the black-fly and we eliminate river blindness. What we've got to do is to find the breeding places of the black-fly and destroy them. They breed in water, so first we must discover which streams are infected.'

He had the *infirmiers* on the lookout for anything that grew or floated in the Yakusu streams on which might be found the eggs of the black-fly. It involved hacking paths through the undergrowth to get to the streams, and workmen from one of the rubber plantations were sent by the manager to do this. It was in the firm's interest to get rid of the scourge that was causing so much ill-health among its work-force, and any practical help in achieving this end was readily provided. The painstaking and tedious task of wading for hours through black mud, searching for the tiny white eggs of the black-fly was undertaken by Stanley and his assistants, and eventually he found some, little clumps of white eggs attached to stones or vegetation in running water. But where did they change into the larvae and pupae from which the adult black-fly would emerge? Where were the breeding places?

By the time he was due for furlough he had not solved the mystery, so he packed up all his copious notes to take with him as he and Mali prepared to return to England again, taking Alastair and Christopher with them. He would continue his research into the disease while at home, in the times when he would be free from preaching engagements. From those records and notes he might get a clue as to the breeding-ground of the black-fly in the Congo. He would also complete the M.D. thesis he had started in Yakusu.

During those months at home he was struck afresh with the ease of life, the cushioning against hardship and illness that he saw all around him, comparing it with the stark and ugly realities confronting the disease-ridden people from whom he had come. He went up and down the country with a note of urgency in his preaching, warning of the consequences of spiritual indolence and selfishness.

'One of the most reprehensible attitudes in the Christian life is enjoying the benefits of salvation and keeping the knowledge to oneself,' he said. 'In the desert, the greatest of all crimes is that of knowing where the water is, and keeping the knowledge to yourself.' Then he added, 'We in this country will lose our faith if we try to keep it to ourselves.'

When furlough ended he returned alone to Yakusu, leaving Mali to see the three boys settled in school before rejoining him. It would be hard for both of them to be without them, but he knew that she would feel it even more keenly than he, and when he received an invitation from the World Health Organisation to attend a conference on river blindness which was to be held just about the time she was due back in Yakusu, he hesitated to accept it. If he were away at the conference, it would mean her being alone in the home that held so many memories just at the time when she would most need his companionship. What should he do? Mali told him. A cable came from her with the words, 'Fully understand. Go ahead,' so he went ahead, and it was there at the conference in Leopoldville that he got the clue he had been searching for. He met a man who had had experience in tracking the larvae of the black-fly.

'You'll probably find it on crabs,' he was told.

'But I've examined hundreds of crabs, and found no single larva or pupa on any of them.'

'Persevere. Examine the crabs in the fastest flowing water—that's where they are most likely to be with the larvae on them. Concentrate on the crabs.'

Stanley concentrated on the crabs. The hacking of paths to the streams continued, the scooping up of crabs into buckets, and the steady scrutiny of each crab. Stanley picked them up with forceps, one by one, and turned them round, upside down, looking for the larvae. Dozens, hundreds of crabs were examined, but at last he found what he was looking for. Here was a crab with the larvae of the black-fly clinging to its body. It was a moment of triumph. At last he had found a stream which was a breeding place. In a way it was only a beginning, but it proved he was on the right track. The stream was carefully marked on the map, and then the search began all over again, until every stream in the area where there were crabs with the black-fly larvae had been entered on the map.

Now came the task of disinfecting the waters. It involved long journeys on foot to reach the headstreams, laborious mathematical computations to calculate the quantity and strength of disinfectant required, and the ingenious use of string and old petrol drums with holes bored in them to produce a Heath-Robinson type of equipment in the absence of the real thing. It involved, too, the initial dismay of the waiting Africans as the first release of the disinfectant seemed to do no more than turn the water milky-white and kill off all the little fish. But the process of disinfecting was continued relentlessly every ten days, and with the steady reduction in the number of flies the river blindness was disappearing.

About this time Noel Barber, a news correspondent from the *Daily Mail* arrived in Yakusu, searching for copy. It was no unusual thing now for journalists as well as Government officials to visit the place which was fast becoming the most famous Protestant mission centre in the Congo, but most of them were from the Continent, not from the British Isles. Mr. Barber knew what would make a good story for his paper, and late in November, 1955, a photo of Stanley examining a crab appeared in it under a headline title of 'The Moment of Victory', with a caption 'Lone Briton seeks to end river-borne scourge'. The story of his fight against the black-fly was graphically described, and he himself was said to be following in the steps of Livingstone and Schweitzer, a blond, handsome medical missionary with a black bag in one hand and a Bible in the other. While he was on the job the newsman had taken pictures of the leprosarium, so Stanley also appeared in an I.T.V. programme, playing the organ at Yalisombo.

Little wonder that the headmaster of Brockley Central School was proud of this celebrated old boy. He followed his career with interest. When he heard that Stanley was returning unexpectedly to England, he decided that the British Broadcasting Corporation ought to hear about it. 'Dr. Stanley Browne is coming home from Congo,' he informed them. 'The man who has brought river-blindness under control in the Belgian Congo.' The B.B.C. decided to follow it up.

The reason for Stanley's return in mid-term to England was a very personal one. For over a year he had been conscious of discomfort in the lower abdomen, and as time went on he realised that his symptoms might mean he had cancer. After consultation with other medicals and with the

B.M.S. leaders, he was urged to return to England as soon as possible for further investigations, and what might prove to be a very serious operation. His return had not been made public, of course, so he was rather surprised when, on arrival home, he was assailed by a series of three telegrams from one of the producers at the B.B.C., asking him to get in touch. They wanted him to appear on the popular programme 'In Town Tonight'.

Stanley had not come home expecting to address any meetings, or be heard on radio, far less to appear on television. There was only a day to spare to fit in the interview, but arrangements were made quickly, and the programme appeared a week before he was due to enter hospital. It proved to be an unusually moving programme, and those who were perhaps most deeply affected by it were the producer himself and his wife. Peter and Sylvia Duncan were, in fact, so impressed by this 'young doctor' just returned from the heart of Africa and by the story he told so simply of his fight with the diseases there, that they were reluctant to lose touch with him. An enormous bouquet of exotic flowers reached his bedside in hospital from 'his friends at the B.B.C.', and before he returned to Yakusu (the operation revealed a tumour that was non-malignant) they had extracted from him the promise to co-operate with them in the project they now had in mind. They wanted to write a book about his work.

It was a surprising request that they made. It is unusual for a missionary's work to be the subject of a book to be distributed in what is known as the secular market. Not everyone approved of the idea, and from Stanley's point of view he would rather do a job than talk about it. However, its publication would make no difference to him, working and travelling far away in Yakusu, and there would be no need to bring his name into it at all. He could just be called 'Bonganga' throughout, and the general public would be none the wiser, medical etiquette would not be infringed, and the only people who would know to whom 'Bonganga' referred were those who knew already what he was doing.

It was agreed, therefore, that Peter and Sylvia Duncan should visit Yakusu the following year to collect material for the book. Stanley himself returned to the Congo as soon as he had recovered from the operation, and took up again his responsibilities as missionary in charge of the work in Yakusu. His brief visit to England had brought him unexpectedly into the limelight in new circles.

In many ways those were exciting days. Yalisombo was achieving international fame, and a variety of visitors arrived at Yakusu, sometimes unannounced, wanting to be taken across to see it and to talk to him. The Governor-General, members of the Belgian Senate, journalists and leprosy specialists from other parts of Africa made their way there, and Mali, doffing the overall she wore for her work in the dispensary, hurried back to the bungalow to make what provision she could for them in the way of light luncheons or soft drinks and cookies. Perhaps the most surprising visitors of all were the producer, actors and actresses, camera men and the technicians who came to shoot pictures for the leprosarium scenes in THE NUN'S STORY, using Yalisombo as the background. With touching courtesy and sympathy they returned a few days later, not to shoot pictures, but to attend one of the special services of thanksgiving for cured leprosy patients who were pronounced symptom-free and ready to be discharged. 'The Grateful Samaritan' service, it was always called, in memory of the leprosy sufferer in the Gospel, the Samaritan who turned back to give thanks, the only one to do so of the ten the Lord healed. 'This is *real*,' the producer whispered to Stanley. He was obviously moved. 'I'd rather be filming this than THE NUN'S STORY . . .!'

It was during this period that Dr. Robert Cochrane visited Yalisombo again, saw Stanley's multitudinous duties, and said to him,

'You ought to concentrate on leprosy.'

'I can't do that,' replied Stanley, rather surprised at the

suggestion. It was only a short time since he had successfully
tackled the problem of river blindness, and there was a
constant war to be waged on other diseases. 'There's too
much to be done in other directions to concentrate on any
one disease. I'm doing what I can.' He was co-operating
with laboratories in London now, frequently despatching to
them specimens of skin containing live leprosy bacilli. To
get everything done he was up each morning before dawn,
as the junior missionaries on the compound noted with
mingled dismay and admiration, conscious that they fell far
short of his standard. 'I couldn't confine myself to leprosy.'

Dr. Cochrane persisted. 'There's much more to be done,
much more,' he said. 'Leprosy—it's a world-wide problem.
More research needed. Leprosy workers everywhere who
ought to be taught what you know. You can't do everything.
You should concentrate on leprosy.'

The words stuck in Stanley's mind, though he tried to
ignore them. As things worked out, they proved to be
prophetic. Nor were they the only prophetic words that
Robert Cochrane spoke.

'The time is short,' he affirmed in 1954, referring to
Africa. 'Independence is in the air, and it is only a matter of
time when the Church, like those of the more advanced
countries now, will want its freedom from outside control.
We forget that in eighty to a hundred years Africa has
advanced to a position which took Europe over a thousand
years. We forget we cannot plan for a hundred years. We
shall be fortunate if foreign missionaries have more than
twenty . . . Rumblings of unrest already come from across
the borders . . .'

As far as Stanley was concerned, the rumblings of unrest
were not confined to the political realm in the Congo, nor even
to the Church there. During the last year or two he had become
the central figure in a Mission controversy. There were diver-
gences of opinion on matters of medical policy. Should the
community health programme inaugurated by Dr. Chesterman and loyally maintained ever since he left now be aban-

doned in order to build up Yakusu hospital as a curative centre? Was not the control of disease and the raising of standards of health and hygiene in the whole district for which Yakusu was responsible of primary importance? Not everyone agreed with him about this; some favoured the concentration of medical resources and personnel in the hospital.

The leprosy programme also came under fire. Some did not approve of Stanley's ideas for developing it. When the Congo government, following Dr. Cochrane's suggestion, proposed that Yalisombo should become an international leprosy research centre with Stanley at its head, the reaction from Mission headquarters was prompt and final. It came by cable. The answer was No.

There were tensions among the Africans, too. As senior missionary Stanley had had to assume responsibility in the church, in which a small group objected to the strict standards of discipline. Mali and he looked at each other wide-eyed when they learned of some of the accusations being levelled against them by this little group, which were being taken to England by visitors who had listened to them. Outwardly things were going very well in every department of the work in Yakusu, and when the time came for the Brownes to leave for furlough, a huge crowd of Westerners and Africans, chief among them the *infirmiers* Stanley had trained, was there at the Stanleyville airport to see them off.

'God speed! Come back soon! See you next year.'

But Stanley and Mali knew in their hearts that they wouldn't be going back in a few months' time. Things seemed to be coming to a head, and they packed, quietly and sadly, not expecting to return. Just before they arrived back in England the book by Peter and Sylvia Duncan entitled *Bonganga* was published. Its closing words seemed to take on a prophetic ring: 'Was he to let others carry on his work at Yakusu and in the forest, and put his experience to the full benefit of leprosy?' No one could forsee then that his fight against leprosy was going to be waged on a much wider scale than if he had remained in the service of the Mission.

It is becoming fashionable to ridicule and sneer at Christian beliefs. Those who uphold Christian standards are pilloried, or politely ignored. Rather than bow before the onslaught, we should take the war into the enemy's camp, graciously, but with deliberation. Before we can battle effectively with any hope of success, however, we must ourselves be well prepared and well equipped—by reading, observation and discussion. In this way we shall be able to help the undecided, the waverers and the decent, uncommitted types among our fellow students . . .

In the midst of the tumbling morals and permissiveness of today, we have a duty to become reasonably well informed about such matters as drugs and drink, of sex and immorality, of heart and organ transplants, and of 'abortion on demand'. These are matters on which every doctor should have informed opinions, and on which he should be able to speak out. I sometimes fear that Christians are more concerned about orthodoxy of belief and its expression than with the matters that weigh heavy on the thoughts of our neighbours.

S.G.B.

(From an address to London medical students on 8 May, 1978)

CHAPTER ELEVEN

Widening horizons

The Brownes had been home for nine months when, after being involved in many anxious, sometimes agonising discussions, they finally decided to resign from the Baptist Missionary Society, although by this time they had been completely vindicated. It was a painful experience, for they had both been associated with the Mission from childhood—Mali, indeed, had been born into it. Their resignations were accepted in April, 1959, to take effect after six months, during which time Stanley would continue his deputation work for the Mission. After that he did not know what he would do.

As the weeks passed he found it increasingly difficult to answer the friendly questions asked about his future.

'That was a most challenging talk you gave us. Thank you so much for coming,' the convenor of the meeting would say, then add,

'When are you going back to the Congo?'

'We shan't be going back.'

'Not going back?' Then, after a surprised pause, the inevitable query, 'What will you be doing, then?'

There was no very satisfactory answer to that question, except to the sort of people who would understand the reply, 'We are waiting for the Lord to show us.' He made tentative enquiries regarding possible employment with the Medical Research Council, the Liverpool School of Tropical Medicine and the London School of Hygiene and Tropical Medicine, but there were no vacancies. He and Mali looked into a future shrouded in mist. They felt very like Christian in *Pilgrim's Progress* as he walked through the Valley of

Humiliation. Never before had they experienced anything like this. They reassured each other that God would not desert them or leave them to find their way alone, but when Stanley was asked to join the Mission to Lepers and go to India, and then offered an appointment as junior lecturer in tropical medicine, they were both conscious that neither of these suggestions was what he was intended to follow. How long was this uncertainty to continue? By July they were both feeling the strain.

During that month, at the time of the Annual Meeting of the British Medical Association in Edinburgh, Stanley was there to speak at a breakfast organised by the Christian Medical Fellowship. It was an occasion that left a lasting impression on at least one of those present who, twenty years later, remembered having been almost moved to tears by his address. It left a lasting impression on Stanley, too, but for a quite different reason. On that very morning a letter had been delivered to the house in Eltham where the Brownes were living temporarily, and Mali had opened it. As she read it, it was as though the mist suddenly lifted to reveal a new, utterly unexpected sunlit view. Here was the right opening at last. This was something to which she knew Stanley would respond with confidence and enthusiasm. Long distance telephone calls were an expense she rarely incurred, but this was an occasion that demanded one.

'Stanley,' she said when she heard his voice at the other end of the line. 'There's a letter for you. It's from the Crown Agents, acting on behalf of the Government of Eastern Nigeria. They're inviting you to succeed Dr. Frank Davey as Senior Leprologist at Uzuakoli. It's quite urgent, they need your reply immediately . . . And, Stanley, the terms include annual leave for us both in England. We'll be able to see the boys each year . . .' There was no mistaking the excitement in her voice, the telegraph wires fairly tingled with it as she read the letter to him, and as he listened his spirits rose. To be in charge of the famous Leprosy Research Unit at Uzuakoli, and of leprosy control throughout the eastern region of Nigeria—what a privilege and what an opportunity! The salary mentioned made him sigh with relief. Governments can afford to pay their employees much more than can missionary societies. No fear now that the boys might have to go short of anything they needed.

'I'll follow it up straight away,' he assured Mali, making notes quickly as he spoke. 'I'll be back home just as soon as I've finished up here. I shall have to hurry to get everything settled and be ready to leave within a month. This is wonderful. Thank God. Goodbye dear.'

The relief was almost overwhelming. It was not so much the sudden lifting of all financial anxiety that brought the easing of inward tension, but the stimulus of again having the sort of job for which he felt qualified and one which opened up new possibilities in a realm of particularly poignant need. 'You should concentrate on leprosy,' Robert Cochrane had said, and a sense of fulfilment came over him as he contemplated doing so.

One month after receiving that telephone call, he was arriving at the airport in Enugu, capital of Eastern Nigeria, the centre of a coal-mining region.

He was glad to be back in Africa again, though in some ways it was a very different Africa from the one he had known in rural Belgian Congo. If the dwellings of brick and corrugated iron were not so picturesque as the wattle and daub hut villages around Stanleyville, they were certainly more hygienic, and the hundred-and-ten-mile drive along tarmac roads compared very favourably with churning over dirt tracks in the Red Devil. On arrival at Uzuakoli, however, he realised that the large compound with its shrubs and trees and spacious lawns, its hospital buildings and school, dormitories and houses for the staff, had the same indefinable atmosphere as that at Yakusu. There was an air of order and purpose about it, and of quiet contentment. As Stanley was welcomed by the man he was to succeed, Dr. Frank Davey, and by his wife, he knew he had met people with whom he felt at one, and whose aims were the same as his own.

The story behind the Uzuakoli Leprosy Hospital was like a rich tapestry into which threads of varied hues had been drawn together. It started in 1927 when a doctor of the Church of Scotland Mission established at Itu, sixty miles from Uzuakoli, a settlement for the many leprosy sufferers who had been coming to his hospital for help. It was the first of its kind in Nigeria. This awakened the British Government to the fact that with the opening up of the country, leprosy, which had up till that time been confined to the rural areas, was now spreading in the towns at an alarming rate. Main roads brought trade and industry, but they encouraged the spread of diseases as well. It was one of the more disturbing effects of progress, and something must be done about it. The Government therefore invited the Methodist Missionary Society to co-operate with it to deal with the situation, and in 1932 Uzuakoli Leprosy Hospital was opened.

In 1936, the year that Stanley had set out for the Congo, Dr. Frank Davey had taken responsibility for the hospital at Uzuakoli, and over the years had also developed a leprosy control programme with over a hundred local treatment centres which covered the entire region, similar in some respects to the dispensaries operated from Yakusu, though confined to treating the one disease.

It was his intense interest in research, however, that had made Uzuakoli of special significance in the world of leprosy. In 1948 it had become the official BELRA research centre in Nigeria, and received grants from the British Government. John Lowe, another eminent leprologist, joined him, and together they undertook the pilot trial of dapsone by mouth for leprosy patients.*

* Drs. Lowe and Davey showed that the expensive drugs derived from dapsone exerted their anti-leprosy effect by reason of the dapsone that was released when the former drugs were broken down in the liver. They therefore gave dapsone at much smaller doses than had been initially prescribed, and obtained good results, as did Stanley Browne in Yalisombo at the same time. This was a most important step in the treatment of leprosy.

The Nigerian Government having created the Nigerian
Leprosy Service, they also took over the Research Unit, and
when Dr. Davey eventually intimated he must leave to
become Medical Secretary of the Methodist Missionary
Society in London, it was the Nigerian Government that
invited Stanley to take his place.

During the three weeks that Stanley spent being introduced to the work by Dr. Davey, the two men found
themselves in complete accord, not only in their attitude
towards leprosy, but in their conviction of their calling.

'God was in Stanley's coming,' wrote Dr. Davey many
years later, 'but it was part of a much wider and extended
picture involving many people over a period of thirty years,
the purpose of which was to change the lot of leprosy
sufferers everywhere. I am quite convinced of this in relation
to myself, but I feel very strongly that what happened was
not thanks to this man or that man, but that we together
offered obedience to the call that came to us, and together
became a powerful instrument in God's hands. This does
not just apply to the Europeans. It applies very strikingly
and wonderfully to the dedicated Nigerians without whom
the whole story from beginning to end would never have
happened.'

Not least among those Nigerians were the leprosy patients
who like Dickie in the Congo willingly offered their bodies
for the trials with new drugs. Dr. Davey was bound to them
by the same indescribable sense of fellowship as was Stanley
bound to Dickie and others away in the Congo. Their
patients had trusted them to try out something that might
prove the way of deliverance from the living death of the
leprosy sufferer—but which might, on the other hand, cause
intolerable pain and in the end prove useless. The doctors
who conducted the trials never forgot those who had trusted
them.

As they talked together, Dr. Davey revealed to Stanley
what had been perhaps his greatest difficulty in alleviating
the lot of the leprosy sufferer in Nigeria.

'It's the stigma.' As in so many parts of the world, leprosy was regarded as a divine punishment for wrong-doing, and the word 'leper' was almost synonymous with the word 'sinner'. The 'leper' was one who had incurred the wrath of the Supreme Being and was therefore beyond the pale. Fear of the physical effects of the disease was no greater than fear of other dread ills that dog mankind. It was the social and psychological consequences of contracting leprosy that filled people with horror. It made them outcasts from society, shunned by their own families, deprived even of compassion.

'I've been fighting the prejudice for years,' Dr. Davey told Stanley, explaining how he had at last succeeded in obtaining permission to have leprosy patients admitted into some general hospitals on occasion. It had been difficult to convince the medical and nursing staffs that it was safe to do so, and the average Nigerian remained apprehensive. The superstitious revulsion persisted, and the sufferer from leprosy was regarded as different from the sufferer from any other disease. He was an outcast.

Stanley nodded. He understood, although it had not been one of the problems in the Congo where, when leprosy isolated its victim, it was entirely for economic reasons. He was unproductive, ate food without doing anything to earn it, so he must go. But elsewhere in the world, as Stanley knew, the social attitude towards the sufferer constituted for him his chief anguish. There were those like Robert Cochrane who had seen that unnecessary distress with eyes of compassionate understanding, and were determined to change it. By being seen to mix freely and fearlessly with leprosy sufferers, by making known the simple facts about the disease, and by using every means they could think of to eliminate the word 'leper', they would change it. For Stanley, too, the fight against the prejudice was to become as demanding as his fight against the disease itself.

Three weeks after Stanley arrived, Dr. and Mrs. Davey left, and he found himself in a situation more favourable than anything he would have thought of choosing for himself. The bungalow he was to occupy was spacious and well-appointed, the garden colourful with flowers and rich with fruit and vegetables; a tennis court and a small swimming pool near-by provided opportunity for physical exercise, and the salary he received would enable him to buy a second-hand car. It would be the first car he had owned. Better still were the opportunities his employment afforded for reading and writing. Except when visiting other lepro-saria he was officially on duty from eight a.m. to two-thirty p.m., seeing patients and supervising laboratory investiga-tions. For the rest of the day he was free. The Nigerian Government made no further demands on him. He could go to his study and work on all those notes he had made on leprosy while in the Congo. 'I was actually being paid for pursuing an engrossing hobby,' he sometimes said.

'Observe. Record. Publish,' Mr. Wakeley had impressed on him at King's, but there had been no time to accomplish much in the way of publishing during those crowded years in Yakusu. He had managed to write a few articles for medical journals, mainly in French, and one or two for the *Lancet*, but they didn't amount to more than a dozen in all. Now he could do what he longed to do, spend six hours a day and more if he liked, on research and reading and writing up the results of his findings. And as he now had a secretary, he would even be spared the time-consuming task of typing out his drafts.

Shortly after he arrived in Uzuakoli he was reading a Lagos newspaper when he came across a news item about a political group in a neighbouring African country pressing for self-government, and chuckled as he saw the heading, 'Mali demands S.G.'. He cut it out and enclosed it in his next letter to Mali thinking that it would be just as true to assert that 'Stanley George demanded Mali'. She had waited in England until the summer vacation was over and the boys back in school before rejoining him. The parting from them this time was going to be easy, even exciting, for within a few months they would be coming out to spend the

Christmas holidays in their parents' new home. The Nigerian
Government would pay their air fares out to Nigeria once a
year, so what with Stanley and Mali having an annual leave
as well, the family's years of long separation were over.
Mali's parents had already had their house in Sutton
converted into two self-contained flats, the lower one now
being available for the Browne family. Everything seemed
to be falling into place, and it had all come about so suddenly
that when he met her at the airport in Enugu it was difficult
to realise only three months had elapsed since the days when
he and she had looked into a future that seemed a complete
vacuum.

Life was just as full now as it had ever been, but with a
difference. The new appointment ushered them into new
circles, academic and governmental, and into new spheres
of Christian activity too. They settled into life in the leprosy
settlement at Uzuakoli as happily and freely as in Yakusu,
attending the Methodist Sunday services morning and
evening at which Stanley preached frequently. Before long
he was asked to become a Methodist local preacher, and he
remembered with a smile the occasions when he had been
turned out of a Methodist Sunday School for bad behaviour.
Not only at Uzuakoli was he in demand as a speaker, but
also at the mission leprosy settlements, Protestant and
Catholic, scattered throughout Eastern Nigeria which he
visited reguarly several times a year. Mali, who never had to
look far afield for something to do, joined the Women's
Institute at Uzuakoli and was elected President almost
immediately. She also began coaching bright patients for
University exams.

One of their main weekly activities was in connection with
the Literary Society of which they became enthusiastic
members. The Society was run by the leprosy patients
themselves, many of whom could speak English, were well-
educated, and eager to extend their knowledge of the outside
world. This sort of mental stimulus, Stanley knew, was as
important in its way as the medical treatment he was giving

them, and it helped to establish friendly relations between him and his patients, building up mutual respect and trust, as his predecessors had done.

'In leprosy you have to be trusted by the patients, otherwise you can't do effective research work. It's not a question of just giving them one shot of penicillin and saying goodbye, but of being with them and understanding them and loving them, and caring for them and treating them to the best of one's ability. This is the way we were able to build up some very happy co-operative efforts with the leprosy patients. Our colleague, Dr. Hogerzeil, a Dutchman, was a tremendous help to us, a fine Christian man with a very good knowledge of leprosy and an excellent attitude towards patients.

'Another colleague was Mr. Fred Hasted, who afterwards became a local organising secretary for the Leprosy Mission in England. He was appointed by the Methodist Missionary Society as the Welfare Officer, and developed an excellent occupational therapy unit, with physiotherapy and vocational training and guidance, in the demonstration garden and in little skills that were saleable, so that when patients left the leprosy settlement they were able to resume life in their villages once again.

'He was also tremendously interested in the school. In those days we had over one hundred children who had come to the leprosy hospital at Uzuakoli because of social, not medical reasons. They had been turned out of school, some of them even turned out of their homes, because they had leprosy. With Mr. Hasted's help and encouragement they were welcomed into the settlement and into the schools.'

These good relations between staff and patients made it possible for Stanley to continue with drug trials as had Frank Davey before him, and ultimately to prove the efficacy of yet another drug with which to continue the fight against leprosy. It was in 1960, when he was home on leave in England, that Dr. Robert Cochrane asked him to come and discuss some new products he was interested in, especially one given the code name of B663. It had been developed by Dr. Vincent Barry at the Dublin Medical Research Laboratories, and after being swallowed it became concentrated in the very cells in the body that took up the bacillus that causes leprosy. The question was, could this drug, B663, be brought into proximity to the leprosy bacilli in these cells, and destroy them?

The discussions, the research into toxicology and animal experiments, the studies, covered hours, days, weeks, but by the time Stanley returned to Nigeria he was confident that it was safe to try the drug on leprosy patients. But which ones? He discussed it with Dr. Hogerzeil.

'We decided on a group suffering from bad lepromatous leprosy who would be going downhill rapidly if they were not treated. We decided it would be ethically correct and justifiable to try the new drug on them. They gladly gave their permission, so with their active and happy co-operation I embarked upon the first trials of this new compound.'

The results were similar to those achieved when he first gave Diasone to Dickie, away in Yakusu. The patients began to get better.

'Dr. Browne,' said the laboratory assistants excitedly as they saw the rapid clinical progress and amelioration in the patients' condition. 'If we ever get leprosy, please try this new drug on us.'

Cautiously, after consultation with Dr. Hogerzeil, Stanley produced a preliminary report which was published in the Leprosy Review, in which he suggested that the drug was active in leprosy.

'We didn't go any further than that. When one embarks, however carefully and prayerfully, on the investigation of a new compound, one is always rather fearful that one will run into toxic complications, or else that one's early claims are not confirmed by others. The therapeutic pathway of leprosy is littered with discarded and disallowed claims of this nature. We mentioned that right from our early studies it seemed to have an anti-inflammatory action in addition to the anti-leprosy activity. It seemed to damp down the reactive episodes in leprosy, and actually prevented a number of patients going into reaction who, on standard treatment with dapsone, would otherwise have done so.

'This, then, was the early work on B663, the drug now known as Lamprene or clofazimine, the best of the second-line drugs in leprosy.'

His name was becoming well known in medical circles the world over now, as he wrote article after article for medical journals. Letters started reaching him from people in faraway places asking questions, wanting to come to Uzua-koli to see the research work and to receive instruction in leprosy. The mail that was delivered to him bore stamps from many countries and the signatories of the letters were very varied, but he was quite unprepared for one which reached him in 1961 in connection with the International Leprosy Congress to be held in Rio de Janeiro in 1963. It was not merely an invitation to attend as a delegate. That would not have surprised him, but to be asked to be Chairman of a workshop on the treatment of leprosy at the Congress was an unexpected honour and also a heavy responsibility. It involved him in a flood of extra work sending questionnaires to leprosy centres all over the world, collating information and maintaining a steady correspondence with other members of the working party. As always, when he had a commission to fulfil, his groundwork was meticulous. He left nothing to chance.

This thorough and painstaking way of his impressed itself on younger colleagues. When the time came to speak he could do so without the notes he had with him. It was as well that he could, for on his first visit to the University at Ibadan the lights went out just as he had started lecturing and the Registrar, with a gasp of dismay, realised that there were not even any candles ready for such an emergency. Before he could send anyone off for them, however, it dawned on him that perhaps they were not necessary. The speaker had continued without a pause, as though nothing had happened, and after the first stir of alarm at the sudden darkness the audience had settled back to listen, spellbound, to this amazing new lecturer.

Dr. Felton Ross (later to become Medical Director of the American Leprosy Missions Inc.) was one of the Area Superintendents whom Stanley, in his capacity as Leprosy Adviser to the Nigerian Government visited from time to time. 'He was very organised, disciplined and hard working, a good observer of clinical signs, meticulously recorded, and a collector of voluminous data on his patients, and information on leprosy from the literature,' Felton Ross observed. 'A man of complete integrity in his research work and in other aspects of life, too.

'As a relatively much younger clinician I found him demanding but encouraging. He was always ready to answer my questions, sometimes with answers that were way above my head, especially in the field of dermatology.'

On one occasion when Stanley was visiting Felton Ross he found his younger colleague facing the sort of crisis any surgeon would dread. A patient on whom he had operated had become so ill with gas gangrene, the result of an infection acquired in the operating theatre, that an amputation was necessary to save his life.

Stanley sensed his distress. 'Don't be discouraged,' he said hearteningly. 'And don't think of giving up surgery because this has happened.' Then he added quietly, 'I know what it's like. I've had similar experiences myself.' Perhaps he was thinking of that night early in his time in Yakusu, when the young mother died on the operating table. He was ready with advice on an even deeper level, as Felton Ross discovered when he had to make an important decision regarding his future. The question that had to be decided was whether he should remain in Nigeria or go to Ethiopia, and he discussed the matter with Stanley, eager to know what he thought about it. If he expected the older man to give him a directive to one place or the other, however, he was disappointed. Stanley rarely committed himself to anything like that. He was a ready listener, believing that it often helped a perplexed person to talk things over with someone else, but he was surprisingly reluctant to give specific advice. In this case what he had to say was never forgotten.

'He got me straight on priorities. He said there was only one thing that really mattered. *What was the Lord's will for me at that time?*'

*   *   *

The year 1963 was a crucial year in Stanley's career, for it launched him onto the world scene as far as leprosy was concerned. It started with a trip sponsored by the World Health Organisation which took him to leprosy research centres not only in Africa, but in India and South-East Asia as well. It was the first time he had been to the East with its swarming cities and ancient civilisations and although he was away less than two months he visited more than twenty centres, including Calcutta and Vellore in India, two in the Philippines, one in Malaysia and The Leprosy Mission's work in Hong Kong. At all these places he lectured and helped the workers with their investigations, at the same time learning what he could from them. It was invaluable preparation for the World Congress to be held in Rio de Janeiro later that year. He was back in Uzuakoli in March, immersed again in the manifold activities there, then to England for the annual leave which included a visit to the Geigy Laboratories in Basle to discuss the new drug B663, back again to Uzuakoli, then in September he set out for what was to prove a turning point in his career.

The International Leprosy Congress held in Rio de Janeiro left little time for viewing the many fine buildings and flourishing industries of the spectacular Brazilian city, and even had there been, Stanley would not have been eager to do so. The five hundred delegates at the Congress included the leading leprosy research workers in the world, and these were the men he wanted to meet, to learn from them and to share what he knew. He met face to face at last the other members of the working group with whom he had been preparing for this occasion by correspondence for two or three years, and with his faculty for remembering faces, names and facts it was easy for him to get into friendly association with them as individuals, right from the start. A number were French-speaking, and his fluency in that language was an added asset. If he had been virtually unknown in the wider field of leprosy when he arrived, by the time it was all over and he had presented his report he had been elected a Councillor of the Association, the first step on the ladder which was to lead to a more strategic position than anything he had ever dreamed of. And at the final session of the great Plenary Congress the one who had been nominated to voice the appreciation and thanks of all the delegates from abroad to their Brazilian hosts was a newcomer, the quiet, friendly Englishman of medium height, medium build, medium colouring, named Stanley Browne.

It had been arranged that he should go on, via Venezuela, to attend a committee meeting of the International Society for Rehabilitation of the Disabled in Carville, Louisiana, U.S.A. The two days he spent in Venezuela with the Director of the Research Clinic in Caracas went happily enough until his arrival at the airport. There he was informed that unless he could provide the Immigration authorities with certificates proving he had discharged all his income tax obligations during his stay in the country, and with police certificates saying he had committed no crime while there, he could not leave.

Unfortunately, he had not been acquainted with these requirements when he was provided by the Venezuelan embassy in London with what was evidently the wrong type of visa for a short stay in the country.

There alone at the airport in a strange country he had to think quickly. It was one of the occasions when friendships came to his aid. He thought of a doctor he had met at the

Leprosy hospital not far away. He found his telephone number, phoned, and to his great relief heard the familiar voice replying to him, 'I'll pick you up in a quarter of an hour.' Within minutes the resourceful doctor was in his car, racing to the airport. A breathless drive along fifteen miles of winding road brought Stanley to Caracas where the doctor had a friend in the Ministry of Finance who had a friend who was able to provide the necessary documents regarding income tax clearance. Then followed another swift drive, this time to the Ministry of Internal Affairs, where the doctor had another friend . . .

The outcome was that Stanley got back to the airport armed with all the certificates required to assure the officials that it was in order to allow him to leave the country, and just in time to catch the last plane that day going by direct flight to New Orleans. There a chauffeur in a peaked cap was waiting for him, took his bag and led him to a waiting car, and an hour later he arrived in Carville, Louisiana where, twenty years before, the first cautious trials of the sulphones had been made. Dapsone, the drug that had brought hope to leprosy sufferers throughout the whole Yakusu area—could he ever forget it?

The committee meeting he was due to attend had already begun when he hurried in with a word of apology to the chairman, Dr. Paul Brand. He had come in at a crucial point in the discussion. A proposition had been made that a centre should be established somewhere in Africa for leprosy rehabilitation and teaching, and the question was—where? Had Stanley failed to reach Carville in time for that committee meeting the whole history of the All Africa Leprosy Training and Rehabilitation Centre might have been different. As it was, he was accepted as being the one best qualified to answer the questions that arose.

Did he think such an institution was needed? Yes.

What, then, did he recommend? What should be the starting structure and what should be the association with other African countries? Could he suggest a country in Africa where there was:

1. A sufficient number of leprosy sufferers to justify such an institution.
2. A medical school and university to ensure academic respectability.
3. A friendly government.
4. The prospect of political stability for at least ten years.

Political stability for at least ten years? Who could foretell that in an Africa that was seething with unrest, where country after country, freed from colonial rule, was plunging into the horrors of civil war? He returned to Uzuakoli to think and pray about the matter before submitting a report outlining his suggestions.

'I cast my mind back and forth over Africa, east, west and central, south and north, and I came to the conclusion there were only two possibilities, one being Kampala, Uganda, the other Addis Ababa, Ethiopia. I could not foresee ten years of political stability in Uganda—how true that proved to be!'

So he wrote his report, suggesting Addis Ababa as being the place most suitable for the establishment of a leprosy centre for all Africa. In 1966, after numerous consultations with various bodies including the Haile Selassie University and the Ministry of Health in Ethiopia, the All Africa Leprosy Training and Rehabilitation Centre was opened on a large compound near Addis Ababa.*

By this time, however, the Brownes were back in England for good. There were several reasons for this move. Dr. Robert Cochrane, on retiring from his position as Director of The Leprosy Study Centre had urged Stanley to take his place. 'From the first time I met you, in Yakusu, I saw you as the one to follow me in this job,' he told him. He was also

---

* The Institution was still functioning in 1976, ten years later.

relinquishing his appointment as Consultant-Adviser to the Ministry of Health, and wanted to suggest that Stanley should succeed him. Almost simultaneously had come another call. Dr. J. Ross Innes, Secretary-Treasurer of the International Leprosy Association had nominated Stanley as his successor and the Council of the Association had unanimously agreed. In both positions he would be required to travel a great deal, but to make his headquarters in London. Reluctant as Stanley and Mali were to leave Africa one further factor weighed sufficiently heavily to tip the balance and bring them to the decision to do so. Their three boys were in their teens, the two younger ones would soon be leaving school to prepare for their chosen careers, while Derek had already started his medical course. The time had come to provide the permanent home background which they had had to deny their children when the way was made so clear that they should serve God and the people of Africa. Mali's parents wanted to move into a bungalow and suggested that Stanley and Mali should take over their house in Sutton. Everything pointed to England now, and after a strenuous deputation tour in the U.S.A. on behalf of the American Leprosy Missions, they returned to their own country and settled in. On 1 January, 1966, Stanley formally took up his position as Director of The Leprosy Study Centre in London's West End.

In that same year, to his intense relief, an organisation with which he was to have increasingly close links changed its name. For years he, along with others who knew the added and unnecessary anguish of leprosy victims because of the stigma attaching to the word 'leper' had been pressing that it should be eradicated. Now it had happened. In 1966 'The Mission to Lepers' disappeared, to emerge under the new name of 'The Leprosy Mission'.

Another of our resources we must learn more and more how to tap in the 80's is prayer—prayer in the sense of listening to God and, in the process, becoming attuned to the divine will and empowered by the divine dynamic. May I pass on four principles I have learned in the school of prayer?

The first: until you've prayed, there's nothing to do; after you've prayed, there's everything to do.

The second: pray as if everything depended on prayer; then work as if everything depended on work.

The third: don't pray for something unless you are willing to obey God if He tells you how to be the answer to your prayers.

The fourth: when we pray, 'coincidences' happen; when we cease praying, they stop happening.

S.G.B.

(Extract from his Presidential address
at the Baptist Union Assembly
April 1980).

CHAPTER TWELVE

On all fronts

'But it's the law, Dr. Browne,' said the Prime Minister. 'It's been the law for hundreds of years. People with leprosy must be sent away to one of the places appointed by the King, and stay there.'

'And give up all hope, human beings condemned to living worse than animals, and die as outcasts,' thought Stanley, looking through the windows of the Prime Minister's Bureau to the clear sharp outlines of the snow-capped mountains around Kathmandu. The vivid memory of what he had seen when he had visited one of those 'places' was disturbing him. The despair, the stench, the degradation had been more horrifying than anything he had witnessed in the Topoke forest years before, when he was in Congo. 'But they've committed no crime, and can't even get any medical treatment,' he said aloud.

The Prime Minister looked distressed. He was a lawyer, trained in India, had travelled abroad, and was sensitive to world opinion. The presence in his country of representatives of the World Health Organisation had not passed unnoticed, and when the British Ambassador had approached him about a leprologist, a Dr. Stanley Browne, who would greatly appreciate an interview with him he had readily agreed to see him. He was sympathetic, too. This problem of people with leprosy was being brought to his attention quite frequently now. The coming into the country of Christian medical missionaries who were willing to treat all kinds of diseases, even the loathed leprosy, had met with genuine approval in some, though not all, official circles. The Prime

Minister listened very attentively to what his English visitor had to tell him about the new methods of treatment that were working such wonders in other countries.

'Leprosy is one of the least contagious of all diseases,' Stanley said. 'We've learned a lot about it in recent years. With the new drugs now available it can be successfully treated in domiciliary fashion by competent medical auxiliaries. If doctors here in Nepal will deal with sufferers from leprosy in the same way as with sufferers from any other illness, the disease can be brought under control. Segregation is quite unnecessary.'

'But the law won't allow it,' the Prime Minister said, shaking his head slowly. 'No doctor is allowed to treat leprosy sufferers except with the King's direct permission. Your Western doctors of The Leprosy Mission have that permission, that's why they can visit the leprosy segregation centres, and treat leprosy sufferers in their hospitals. But for doctors all over Nepal to have people with leprosy coming to their clinics for treatment like anyone else—it's against the law. Only the King can give permission to change the law.'

'Yes, I realise that,' said Stanley. 'I understand that it's not easy to change an age-old law.' Then he said rather deliberately,

'But can't the law be re-interpreted?'

'Re-interpreted?' The lawyer in the Prime Minister fastened on the word, and he looked at Stanley with quickened interest. 'Why, yes. That's a possibility. Re-interpret the law. Dr. Browne,' he said firmly as he stood to terminate the interview. 'It's impossible to change the law, but I promise you I'll bring the matter before the Cabinet, and if it is possible the law shall be re-interpreted. Then anyone qualified as a doctor will be able to treat leprosy openly, with the backing of the Government.'

Stanley walked away with a light step. He had come to Nepal to take part in a seminar organised by the W.H.O. for missionary doctors and Nepalese provincial medical officers, but he knew that something had been achieved in a realm beyond that of medical science by that visit to the Prime Minister. To re-interpret the law regarding leprosy might take months, even years, but he was confident now that a move would be made in that direction.

In his new career as world traveller in the fight against leprosy, he was constantly being confronted with the inherent prejudice with which not only the disease, but also the sufferer, was viewed. Even with the resources now available for effective medical treatment, the problem of providing it remained. It was one thing to have the drugs and the expertise to effect a cure. It was another thing to obtain the co-operation necessary to get the drugs to the patient, and in many countries this proved to be the more difficult problem.

'If you were in my position, how would you use your leprosy budget?' the Minister of Health of one eastern country asked him as they sat together at lunch.

Stanley's face was rather grim as he answered. He had been deeply moved, both by compassion and by anger, as he had seen the way in which leprosy sufferers were ostracised and neglected in this by no means backward country. The State, it seemed, was doing very little for them beyond putting the burnt-out, hopelessly deformed cases into dreary institutions in which to end their unhappy days. The best leprosaria he had seen were those run by Christian missions, Catholic and Protestant, but those in charge were hampered by the general atmosphere which amounted almost to hostility, of officials and public alike. When patients were cured, pronounced clear of the disease, they went out fearfully into a world that would have none of them. The stigma remained. Leprosy!

'What would I do if I were in your position?' Stanley said, looking his questioner straight in the eyes. 'I would spend one third of my budget on education.'

'On education?' The Minister was obviously surprised. 'Not on reconstructive surgery or something like that?'

'No. On education. And I'd start with the doctors.' The Minister of Health was a doctor of medicine, and also of philosophy. He could not fail to realise that what was being said applied to him as well as to others. 'I'd start to educate the doctors, teach them what leprosy really is, that it can be treated like any other disease—and that those who contract it are ordinary human beings, like you and me.'

He paused a minute, then continued. 'And after the doctors I'd try to educate the politicians.' His host came into that category also. He did not usually speak so bluntly, but the situation, he felt, warranted it. He had seen too many intelligent young people with despair in their eyes and deformities that they could have been spared but for the prejudiced indifference of public opinion. If well-educated Ministers of Health were content to remain in ignorance of the means whereby tens of thousands of their fellow-countrymen could be cured of leprosy, Stanley saw no reason for paying them compliments.

Some months later he was in that country again, and his remarks were remembered. Had he revised his estimate on the leprosy budget? he was asked.

'Yes, I have,' was the prompt reply. 'From what I have seen now on this visit, I would raise the proportion to one half. I would start with educating the doctors and the politicians, then go on to those in the media, the opinion-formers, then to community leaders and all those concerned with the administration of this country—this economically advancing country. I'd spend half my leprosy budget on changing public opinion.'

If he had remained a missionary doctor in Africa, he reflected, his views on the subject would have been just the same, but no one would have paid any attention to them. His new status gave him a new authority. The expressed opinion of the Secretary-Treasurer of the International Leprosy Association, the consultant adviser on leprosy to the British Government, soon to be Chairman of the Expert Leprosy Committee of the W.H.O., and the one to whom governments in many developing countries were applying for advice on their leprosy programmes, could not be ignored.

Even His Holiness the Pope was willing to listen to him. This came about when he was visiting Rome, and was unexpectedly summoned to the Palace of the Prince of the Order of Malta, where he learned that he was to be invested with the Commander's Cross of the Order. The fact that he was known to be a Protestant and a Baptist made no difference. He was accepted on the basis of his world-wide services to sufferers of leprosy, rendered in the Name of Christ, and on this basis he gladly received the honour.

The following day an even more surprising summons reached him—this time to the Vatican. In an audience with Pope Paul, during which his command of French facilitated conversation, Stanley had the opportunity to explain that the disease called leprosy in the Bible was not the same as the disease known by the same name in the world today. He had made an exhaustive study of the clinical characteristics of leprosy as outlined in the Book of Leviticus, and found them quite different from those produced by *Mycobacterium leprae*. The conversation was brief but cordial, and though Stanley stopped short at actually kissing the Papal finger it was due to no lack of respect for the gracious man who wore the Papal gown.

He understood now why those strange storms of his last months with the B.M.S. had resulted in his resigning from the Mission and why, when he returned to England from Uzuakoli he had failed to obtain a consultant post for which he knew he was well qualified. He would have been required to run a weekly clinic for tropical dermatology had he been appointed, and would have been precluded from taking the frequent journeys abroad which had become the pattern of his life. The influence he exerted to alleviate the sufferings of leprosy victims by striving to reduce the stigma that had branded them was as important as the medical knowledge that he could impart. In the fight against leprosy the two went hand in hand, and had to be used in nearly every country he visited.

. . . Even in England.

The headquarters of The Leprosy Study Centre was situated in London, in an unpretentious second-floor flat in one of the tall, narrow houses of Wimpole Street. Stanley let himself in here about eight-twenty a.m. each day when he was in England, having travelled up to Victoria on the seven twenty-five a.m. from Sutton. His colleague, Dr. Douglas Harman, and his secretary (when he had one) usually found him in his book-lined office among bundles of bulging files, going through his mail, when they arrived. It was here that he met medically, from time to time, men and women who had contracted leprosy abroad. Some were immigrants, some were people who had lived overseas for long periods, and as they climbed the quiet, carpeted stairs up to the flat many had the vaguely apprehensive feeling that assails people when they go to see a strange doctor for the first time.

One day a tall, neatly dressed Englishman of middle age arrived at the door of the flat and Stanley, who was expecting him, opened the door, invited him in, shook his hand and led him into his office. 'Please sit down there,' he said, indicating the seat opposite his desk. Receiving no reply he glanced at his visitor, and to his amazement saw that the man was in tears.

'Excuse me,' said his visitor brokenly, pulling out a handkerchief and quickly dabbing his eyes. Then he went on in a low voice to explain himself. 'You know I'm a leper— yet you shook my hand. You're the first doctor, knowing what I've got, who has done that. You shook my hand . . .'

'You're mistaken about yourself,' Stanley replied quickly. 'You're not a leper. It's a word I never use. You've simply contracted a mild form of a disease called leprosy. Quite similar to tuberculosis in some ways, though not nearly so contagious. You're my patient, and the treatment I'm going to give you will cure you. That's all.' He smiled reassuringly.

Stanley and his colleague had never avoided shaking

hands with their leprosy patients, but after that little episode a subtle change came over their attitude. When they went each month to examine patients in the little Hospital of St. Giles, near Chelmsford in Essex, the only leprosy hospital in England, they made a point of standing up and greeting each patient with a hearty handshake before turning to the records and proceeding with the examination.

Visitors to the flat in Wimpole Street were comparatively few, but telephone calls as well as letters were frequent, and some led to unusual experiences. As he lifted the receiver one day Stanley heard a woman's voice speaking.

'Can you give me the name and address of a firm that could supply a million tablets of dapsone, please?'

'Yes, I can,' he replied, and proceeded to do so. 'But may I ask who is calling and for whom the tablets are needed?' He was intrigued. A million tablets of dapsone would be sufficient to treat a very large number of leprosy patients, and he wondered where they were.

'I'm phoning on behalf of Mother Teresa of Calcutta,' was the reply. 'The tablets are needed for the lepers her missionaries are treating.'

Stanley drew a sharp breath.

'Oh, please forgive me, but we don't use that word "leper" now. It's too hurtful to the people who have contracted leprosy. We refer to leprosy sufferers. I very much hope,' he added, 'that the tablets will be used properly, and in the right dosage.'

The outcome of that telephone call was one of the outstanding experiences in his colourful life. Mother Teresa invited him to Calcutta, where he spent three days living in a men's hostel and teaching nearly one hundred nurses in the leprosy hospital by a busy railway track.

'I've never had more eager listeners. They drank in everything I told them. Most of them were well educated and came from the upper crust of Hindu society. Some of the men had given up very well-paid jobs to serve "the poorest of the poor". Their dedication would put many of us to shame. It was my privilege to add some medical knowledge and competence to their enthusiasm and devotion.'

When the three days' teaching was over he received a request that surprised him. Although it was known that he was a Protestant, he was invited to preach at Mass on the following Sunday.

'I gladly agreed. Most of us would have called the service Holy Communion, or the Lord's table, or the Lord's supper. Some would call it the Eucharist. They called it the Mass. To me, it was an occasion when believers from different traditions met their Lord in the breaking of bread and the sharing of the wine, as we together remembered the Lord's death "till He come".

'I gave a simple Gospel exposition. They followed with rapt attention. Then they sang "Something beautiful for God", words that had made a deep impression on Malcolm Muggeridge when he visited Calcutta. A memorable experience.'

*   *   *

When Stanley returned from a trip abroad he went straight to work. It was no unusual thing for him to arrive a few minutes' late for a committee meeting with an apologetic explanation that his plane had touched down behind schedule at Heathrow. If he had no other engagement he went straight to Wimpole Street, where he made a point of knocking at his secretary's door, putting his head round it and saying cheerily, 'Reporting for duty.' It was a way of not only telling her he was back, but of learning if anything had happened during his absence. One day, as his head came round the door, she looked up from her typing and said,

'Oh, the Queen's been asking after you.'

Stanley looked at her suspiciously. 'You're pulling my leg,' he said.

'No, it's true. The Queen's secretary phoned to see if you would go to lunch with Her Majesty at Buckingham Palace.

She's holding a lunch for distinguished people in various walks of life, and a personal invitation will be coming to you.'

Stanley's eyebrows went up, and he gave her a quizzical grin. Apart from the occasion when he was invested with the O.B.E in 1966 he had never been to Buckingham Palace.

'What date is it to be?' he asked.

'Tuesday, 12 July.'

He looked at his diary and frowned. 'I've got to be in Oxford that day, at the International Congress of Christian Physicians . . .'

That Congress represented to him a realm which was preeminent. He had maintained his links with Christian medical organisations throughout his career. While in Nigeria he had been a prime mover in founding the Christian Medical Fellowship there, and now that he was settled in England had responded readily to an invitation to chair its Overseas Service Committee. Some of the journeys he made abroad were to conduct seminars sponsored by The Leprosy Mission. The International Congress of Christian Physicians at which he was to be one of the speakers, therefore, was not something he would lightly put aside. On the other hand, an invitation to lunch with his reigning monarch was not only a high honour, but was even in the nature of a royal command.

'I will gladly accept the invitation to lunch with Her Majesty,' Stanley told Her Majesty's secretary over the phone. Then he added, 'But I must be in Oxford by five o'clock that afternoon.' That should present no difficulty, he was assured, as the royal luncheons only lasted a couple of hours. So at the time appointed Stanley alighted from the taxi that had taken him to Buckingham Palace.

'Perhaps we ought to announce you as the King of Leprosy,' said one of the ushers smilingly as he waited in the ante-room. Stanley thought that plain 'Mr. Leprosy' would be even more appropriate. But it was simply as 'Dr. Stanley

Browne' that he went in to have lunch with Her Majesty the Queen.

He greatly enjoyed it. His monarch, he discovered, knew quite a lot about leprosy, while her phenomenal memory enabled her to talk to him about Nigeria as she recalled details of her visit there some years before, even remembering the song with which she had been welcomed.

He enjoyed even more the State banquet he attended some years later, for Mali was with him then. No social occasion was ever quite complete for him without her.

'What a thrill to be present at Buckingham Palace on such an occasion, to meet again Sir Clement and Lady Chesterman, our predecessors at Yakusu, and various members of the Zaire delegation. Eleven members of the Royal Family were sitting at the top table, with President and Madame Mobutu.' After the banquet they talked with the Queen Mother, the Duke and Duchess of Kent, Princess Alice of Athlone, all of whom had had association with leprosy organisations. 'A most delightful evening with uninhibited conversation and friendliness. We will never forget it.'

The frequent journeys that took him away from home made the occasions when they could be together stand out the more vividly, and the highlight for them both during those years of the 1970s was the visit they paid to the new country of Zaire which they had known so well in the days when it was the Belgian Congo.

Seventeen years had passed since the farewell from Yakusu, when scores of Africans had gathered to see them off and sing with deep emotion, 'God be with you till we meet again.' During that time the Simba rebellion with all its attendant horrors had swept over the whole area, and Stanley and Mali wondered what they would find, who would be left of the many Africans they had known. As the plane touched down on the runway at Kisangani (Stanley-ville) they were the first to reach the door of the plane and begin to descend the gangway. Security was obviously tight, with many soldiers around, and they were surprised to see three civilians approaching the plane across the tarmac. Then Stanley saw that they were waving, and suddenly he recognised them.

'It's Dickie!' There he was, hurrying forward with a broad smile on his face, the same strong, purposeful Dickie who had willingly offered his body for the trials with dapsone.

'Dickie! and Laurie!' After that they seemed to be carried from one exciting re-union to the next. A guard of honour of *infirmiers*, embraces from teachers and pastors, women jostling to speak to Mali.

'*Bonganga!* Do you remember me?'

'*Mama!* You taught me in school!'

Bonganga! Bonganga! Mama!

The biggest church in Kisangani packed to the doors, with Laurie leading the choir in the Hallelujah Chorus. 'You taught me to do it, *Bonganga*.'

And the tales they heard! Courage, and deliverances, and long endurance. That group of leprosy sufferers who, under the leadership of one man of dauntless faith, Lombale, dug a deep pit when they heard that the Simbas were coming, lined it with corrugated iron and mackintosh sheeting, stacked into it all they could carry of the medicines and laboratory equipment from the Government hospital, covered it all over with eighteen inches of earth and planted the whole field with manioc before melting away into the forest.

Five hundred of them, living off the forest for two years, losing track of time but remembering to keep one day in seven for worship. Reading the Bible. Praying.

When the tide turned at last and the Simbas were driven out, the leprosy sufferers slowly crept back to their wrecked hospital, and saw that the manioc field was ready for reaping. And when the pit was opened, not a piece of glass that they had hidden was broken, the microscopes were in good order, and the tins containing thousands and thousands of dapsone tablets were dry as a brick from the kiln.

Not all the tales they heard were triumphant, though. The

Simbas had left deep scars on minds as well as on bodies, maiming them for life. There were many widows and fatherless children. The land itself still seemed to be shuddering from the blows it had received, with fields untended, fallen trees left to rot, the jungle encroaching. The flourishing, well-kept Mission compound Stanley and Mali had known at Yakusu now showed signs of neglect. As for the efficient medical service, with its network of dispensaries spreading over thousands of square miles, it had been almost completely disrupted.

'The leprosy patients?'

'The dispensaries were closed. No more medicine. Lists of patients' names destroyed . . . There are again many people with leprosy . . .' The Government was trying to build the medical service up again (one half of their medical staff were those who had been trained at Yakusu) but it would take years to restore it to its former effectiveness. And because the killing diseases had to be dealt with first, leprosy continued largely unchallenged to claim its victims into a living death.

This discouraging situation, Stanley knew, was not confined to one area. The story was the same in all the countries that had been paralysed by civil war. He studied the statistics that were published by various governments, and knew that when numbers of leprosy patients were recorded they referred to those who were being treated. What of the vast numbers of people with the disease who were still hiding it, or living in the remote areas where statistics were hard to obtain, and to which medical services had not yet reached? He thought of some of the lonely places he visited where medical missionaries, many of them women, were providing the only treatment within hundreds of miles that would deal with leprosy.

He continued his travels far and wide, to organise and attend conferences, conduct seminars, and by his insistence and urgency impress on his listeners the necessity to look for and recognise the disease in its earliest stages, then to treat it. 'Treatment is easy. Diagnosis is everything,' he reiterated. Articles and booklets poured from his pen, some of them written while he was travelling. His exceptional command of English, both in writing and speaking, added quality to all that he produced.

He was constantly on the go. On more than one occasion Mali met him at Heathrow with a suitcase of winter clothes, exchanging it for the one with which he had just returned from a visit to the tropics. They had a few hours together at the airport, then he was off again. Belgium, India, Thailand, Cairo, Paris, Germany, Addis Ababa, Korea, Rome, Lesotho, Davos, Zambia, Mexico, Lisbon . . .

He stayed in a variety of homes, east and west, north and south, adapting himself to differing backgrounds without difficulty. The young people in those homes soon lost any awe they might have had of this eminent person.

'Take this as a motto,' he said in parting to the youngest daughter of one of his hosts. ' "Work hard, play hard, pray hard." '

He grinned at her quick retort, 'I'll take the middle one, and leave the first and the last to you, Dr. Browne.' He certainly didn't leave much time for the middle one, he acknowledged to himself later on. He didn't know if he'd even be able to fit in a Saturday afternoon to go blackberrying with Mali this year . . .

It was during a year when he made about sixteen overseas tours that he received the first intimation of another turn in the course of his life, one of which he had never thought. From the time when he became a medical student his witness and discipleship to Jesus Christ as Lord had been almost entirely in the context of medicine. As a missionary doctor he had been invited to preach when on furlough from Yakusu or Uzuakoli. As a doctor and a leprologist he had served on many committees. By virtue of his distinctive role in leprosy he had found himself speaking at meetings all over the world, and had not hesitated to take his stand as a Christian while doing so. So when one of his friends in The Leprosy Mission asked him one day,

'Have you ever considered yourself as President of the Baptist Union?' he had an immediate answer.

'President of the Baptist Union? Never!' he said. 'I've never even thought of it.'

'Well, will you allow me to find twenty-five members of the Baptist Union who would be willing and ready to nominate you?'

Stanley stared at him in surprise, and his friend went on, 'I believe you've got a message for the denomination at this time.'

'Well,' said Stanley rather slowly, 'if God wants me there, and I have a message, I'd be willing. All right. You can go ahead.'

'But I don't think you stand a chance of being elected, Stanley,' said Mali frankly when he told her about it. 'You're not sufficiently well known among Baptists. Most of them have never even heard of you.'

She was in a position to know. Since their return from Nigeria she had again become an active member of the denomination and was, in fact, President of the Baptist Women's League this very year. She had been invited to Buckingham Palace because she was the wife of Dr. Stanley Browne, but she had been elected President entirely on her own merits, as Stanley himself recognised when on one occasion he was on the same platform with her, and was introduced by the chairman as being 'Mrs. Browne's husband'. He told the story against himself more than once. He wasn't known to many in the Baptist Union.

'You're right, Mali,' he said. 'Very few of them know me. I shan't be elected.'

* * *

But they were both wrong.

In March, 1979, a letter was sent out in the usual way to every member of the Baptist Union Council and to every

Baptist Church in membership with the Union, containing biographical details of three men who were being nominated for the Vice-Presidency of the Union. As everyone knew, the one elected would automatically become president in the following year. One of those nominated was:

BROWNE, Dr. Stanley George, C.M.G., O.B.E., M.D., F.R.C.P., F.R.C.S., D.T.M. He had been a Baptist Missionary Society missionary in Zaire for nearly a quarter of a century, and was a member of the Sutton Baptist Church, one of the Baptist Men's Movement, and of the B.M.S. Medical Advisory Committee. For the last twenty years, however, his interests and activities had evidently ranged over a much wider field, and with what appeared to be a comparatively limited experience and association with the Baptist Union, it might have been expected that he would gain the least number of votes. In the event, he gained the largest number. Not a few of those who voted for him had remembered hearing him speak on deputation years ago, when he was a missionary doctor home on furlough. He'd had a message then. Surely he had one now?

In April, 1979, Stanley knew that in April 1980 he would become President of the Baptist Union of Great Britain and Ireland, the first medical doctor to occupy that position.

To occupy this new office was evidently in the plan for his life, and he prepared for it with zest. There was something very fitting in being brought back into the heart of the denomination into which he had been born both naturally and spiritually, just as he was fulfilling his three score years and ten. His mind went back to the day of his baptism, 22 November, 1922. He still had in his possession the simple little card given to him to commemorate the occasion, with the words on it *The Lord shall guide thee continually and satisfy thy soul*. Nearly sixty strenuous but satisfying years had passed since then, in the course of which he had received many honours, mainly in recognition of his services in the field of leprosy.

He had appreciated the honours, but he knew that the

battle he had been fighting on behalf of the leprosy victims wasn't over yet. The ebb and flow of politics, the devastations of civil war, the shortage of money and even more of man-power, left all too many sufferers washed up, as it were, on isolated beaches where no medical help was available. Of the estimated 15,000,000 leprosy cases in the world, only one-third were receiving any treatment at all—and how many more were there who had not even been discovered, who weren't included in those general statistics?

Whatever unexpected position he was called upon to fill, he knew he couldn't forget them. In the very week before he was due to take office at the General Assembly of the Baptist Union he would be travelling abroad on their behalf. Already he was looking ahead to 1983, for he was responsible for planning the International Leprosy Congress to be held in Delhi that year. But meanwhile, there was this year in England, as President of the Baptist Union. 'I believe you've got a message for us at this time,' his friend had said, and the thought of his coming opportunities was frequently in his mind.

'With Christ into the 80's' should be his rallying cry, and he would ensure that no one was left in any doubt but that the Christ of Whom he spoke was the historical Christ of the Gospels, Son of the Living God, moving by His Spirit in the world today. He had plenty of examples to quote from what he had seen in his travels. 'Expect great things from God: attempt great things for God' had been one of the inspirations of his own life, and he would try to convey the same inspiration to others.

He sat down, pulled out his pen, and with the help of two bulging folders of 'thoughts' accumulated over the previous months, started to write the first draft of his Presidential address.

Epilogue

I pushed open the door of The Leprosy Mission and walked in with the proofs. 'Here it is,' I said, sitting down in Charles Attwater's bright, airy office and pulling the bundle out of my bag. 'Stanley Browne's story.'

'I saw him only yesterday, at the Leprosy Study Centre,' said Charles, swinging round in his swivel chair. Wimpole Street is only about ten minutes walk from Portland Place, and he had often dropped in there. 'There he was, sitting writing in an empty room. It was his last day there. The files, the furniture, the pictures, the microscopes – all gone. No one to take the place of himself and Dr. Harman, so the place is being closed. Pretty stark it looked, too. Sad . . .'

I nodded silently, thinking of the people all over the world who had looked to that Centre, writing anxiously about their leprosy problems. To whom would they turn now? Everything was being dispersed to various centres, where the work would be carried on, in other ways.

'It won't be the same,' I said. 'But he can't go on for ever.' I remembered something he had told me once, that every morning when he awoke he murmured, 'Thank you, Lord, for another day of borrowed life.' At three score years and ten he looked at it like that.

'He's not finished yet, though,' said Charles with a chuckle. 'Off with Mali to Canada at the end of the week, speaking all over the country for The Leprosy Mission, and then attending the Baptist World Alliance. He'll be preaching a lot of sermons this year. I asked him if he managed to bring leprosy into them, and he said, "Always! Can't get it out of my system!"'

I looked round the office with its maps and its charts and

its pictures of leprosy sufferers, and asked how the work was going, what was the general situation regarding in the world today.

'We're barely keeping up with it,' was the somewhat sombre reply. 'The World Health Organisation has difficulty in getting accurate statistics, particularly from the Third World countries, where the prevalence of the disease is higher. There are probably fifteen million people with leprosy in the world today, and only about a third of them getting the treatment that can heal them.'

'What is the hold up?' I asked. 'What is the greatest need? Money? Equipment? Medicines?'

Charles shook his head. 'No, it's not so much money – it's men. Doctors who are prepared to relinquish a place in modern medicine here in the West, with all its opportunities for research, and go into the isolation, physical and intellectual, of living in a leprosy situation. It's asking a lot to expect a young doctor on the threshold of his career to do that.'

But Stanley Browne did. . . .

Prizes etc. for Leprosy

1970   Medal, Royal African Society.
1975   Stewart Prize for Epidemiology, British Medical Association.
1977   Ambuj Nath Bose Prize in Tropical Medicine, given by the Royal College of Physicians, Edinburgh.
1978   J. N. Chowdury Gold Medal, Calcutta.
1979   Damien-Dutton Award.
1979   Special Appreciation Prize, Nihon Kensho-Kai, Japan.
1979   Honorary Foreign Member, Royal Academy of Medicine of Belgium.
      Honorary member of professional bodies in many countries.

Honours

1948   Chevalier de l'Ordre Royal du Lion.
1958   Officier de l'Ordre de Léopold II.
1965   O.B.E.
1976   C.M.G.
1976   F.K.C. (Fellow of King's College, London).
1978   Fellow of King's College Hospital Medical School.
1980   Commandeur de l'Ordre de Léopold.

Appointments

1966–78   Secretary-Treasurer, and
1978–   Secretary of the International Leprosy Association.
1966–78   Medical Consultant, The Leprosy Mission.
1966–80   Honorary Consultant Physician, University College Hospital, Hospital for Tropical Diseases.

1966 –73   Medical Secretary, LEPRA, and Editor *Leprosy Review*.

1966–80   Honorary Consultant Physician, Hospital and Homes of St. Giles.

1966   Honorary Consultant Physician, Order of Charity.

1966   Member, Medical Commission, ILEP.

1971–4   Chairman, Medical Commission, ILEP.

1972–4   President, Christian Medical Fellowship.

1975   Member, Executive Committee, Dr. Schweitzer's Hospital Fund.

1977   Chairman, World Health Organisation 5th Expert Committee on Leprosy.

1977–9   President, Royal Society of Tropical Medicine and Hygiene.

1978–   President, Ludhiana British Fellowship.

1979–82   President, International Association of Physicians to the Overseas Services.

1980–   Member of Council, and of Executive Committee, Hospital and Homes of St. Giles.

Lectureships

1967   A. B. Mitchell Memorial Lecture, Belfast.

1974   Godfrey Day Lecture, Dublin.

1974   Kellersberge Memorial Lecture, Addis Ababa.

1978   Rendle Short Memorial Lecture, Christian Medical Fellowship.

1978   J. N. Chowdury Oration, Calcutta.

1978   Gandhi Memorial Lecture, New Delhi

Also by

Phyllis Thompson

CHINA: THE RELUCTANT EXODUS

The untold story of the withdrawal of the China Inland Mission from China.

The most significant period in the history of modern missions was in the five years following World War II, when the door closed on nearly one quarter of the world's population as China, the largest 'mission field' in the world, came under a Communist government.

For over a century, it had been possible, if often dangerous, for western missionaries to enter the country and preach where they would. By the end of 1950 all that had changed. Most Protestant missionary societies had withdrawn already, and now the largest, the China Inland Mission, decided that open Christian witness was impossible under Communism. The mission must withdraw.

Had the decision come too late?

The story of those years, unrevealed at the time for fear of repercussions on those left in China, is now told.

'*A moving and treasured record.*' – *Church Times*

Phyllis Thompson

THE RAINBOW OR THE THUNDER

'Their only aim was to serve the African community, to help educate them and to tell them of Jesus,' a mission spokesman told the newspaper correspondents. On June 23rd, 1978, mutilated bodies, including a three-week-old baby, were found lying on the edge of a cricket pitch at the Emmanuel Secondary School, Vumba, a lonely out-post in Rhodesia's Eastern Highlands, three miles from the Mozambique border. The missionaries and their families were all from the Elim Pentecostal Church.

Three men, six women and four children were bayonetted or clubbed to death. The children were under seven. Less than a year before the school had been moved 70 miles to the south to Vumba.

What keeps missionaries at their post despite the evident danger? Phyllis Thompson asks the question with understanding and sympathy, as she uncovers a story of commitment and dedication reminiscent of the book of Acts.